Child Development

Jean Marshall and Sue Stuart

Heinemann Educational Publishers
Halley Court, Jordan Hill, Oxford, OX2 8EJ
a division of Reed Educational & Professional
Publishing Ltd.
Heinemann is a registered trademark of Reed
Educational and Professional Publishing Ltd.

OXFORD MELBOURNE AUCKLAND
JOHANNESBURG BLANTYRE GABORONE
IBADAN PORTSMOUTH NH(USA) CHICAGO

Text © Jean Marshall and Sue Stuart, 2001
First published in 2001

05 04 03 02 01
9 8 7 6 5 4 3 2 1

British Library Cataloguing in Publication Data
A catalogue record for this book is available from the
British Library

ISBN 0 435 42052 6

Original illustrations © Heinemann Educational
Publishers, 2001
Designed, illustrated and typeset by Hardlines
Picture research by Elisabeth Savery
Printed and bound in Spain by Edelvives

Acknowledgements

The authors and publishers would like to thank the
following for the use of copyright material: Boots for
the material on p. 63; The Department of Health for
the website material on p. 67; The Department of
Social Security for the material on p. 105; Gingerbread
for the website material on p. 108; HMSO for the
material on pp. 99 and 120. Crown Copyright material
is reproduced under Class Licence Number
C01W00141 with the permission of the controller of
HMSO and the Queen's Printer for Scotland;
Knowsley Borough Council for the material on p. 101;
The National Citizens Advice Bureaux for the
material on p. 108; OCR for the exam material on
pp. 122–3 and 126. Reproduced with the kind
permission of OCR.

Cover photograph by ACE Photo Agency.

The publishers would like to thank the following for
permission to use photographs: John Birdsall Photo
Library on p. 100; Gareth Boden on pp. 44, 74, 103;
Mark Boulton on pp. 7, 29, 31, 46, 47, 56, 61, 84, 102;
Mark Boulton/CEC on pp. 29, 31, 46, 80, 119;
Corbis/Reflections Photo Library on p. 37; Cosatto
on p. 31; Early Learning Centre on p. 84, 85;
Format/Joanne O'Brien on p. 106; Format/Lisa
Woollett on p. 99; Sally and Richard Greenhill/Sally
Greenhill on pp. 20, 23, 26, 44, 60, 62, 78, 95, 96, 97;
JJMB on pp. 19, 46; Mother and Baby Picture
Library/Nick Cole on p. 55; Mother and Baby Picture
Library/Ian Hooton on pp. 28, 35; Mother and Baby
Picture Library/Ruth Jenkinson on p. 26; Mother and
Baby Picture Library/Eddie Lawrence on p. 22;
Mother and Baby Picture Library/Paul Mitchell on
p. 36; Science Photo Library on p. 56; Science Photo
Library/Mark Clarke on pp. 66, 93; Science Photo
Library/Deep Light Productions on p. 21; Science
Photo Library/Stevie Grand on pp. 37, 72; Science
Photo Library/John Greim on pp. 28, 37; Science
Photo Library/Ruth Jenkinson/MIDIRS on pp. 27, 94;
Science Photo Library/Maximilian Stock Ltd on p. 18;
Science Photo Library/Faye Norman on p. 33; Science
Photo Library/Chris Priest on pp. 70, 117; Science
Photo Library/Saturn Stills on p. 68; Science Photo
Library/Ron Sutherland on p. 98; Science Photo
Library/Sheila Terry on p. 63; Science Photo
Library/Geoff Tompkinson on p. 36; Science Photo
Library/Hattie Young on pp. 32, 110; Gerald
Sunderland on pp. 34, 35, 38, 39, 40, 41, 42, 75, 81, 86,
87, 88, 92, 110, 111, 112, 113, 124.

The publishers have made every effort to trace the
copyright holders, but if they have inadvertently
overlooked any, they will be pleased to make the
necessary arrangements at the first opportunity.

Tel: 01865 888058   www.heinemann.co.uk

Contents

Introduction

This book has been written to meet the specification requirements for the OCR GCSE in Home Economics (Child Development).

The specification

The specification seeks to encourage an understanding of the overall needs of young children and the social and environmental influences that affect their development in a contemporary, changing and multicultural society. Throughout the course you will have the opportunity to:

+ increase your knowledge and understanding of human needs, the interdependence of individuals and groups, and the influence of social, cultural and economic factors
+ increase your awareness of the implications for Home Economics of rapid technological changes, the use of ICT and the growth of scientific knowledge and understanding, and to develop your ability to respond effectively to such changes
+ foster your critical and analytical approach to decision making and problem solving
+ develop the knowledge and skills required for the effective and safe management of relevant resources.

You will be assessed in two ways. You will have to do internal assessment (coursework) for up to 50 per cent of the marks. You will also have to do a written examination at the end of the course for up to 50 per cent of the marks.

How to use this book

The book is divided into the following units:

1 Parenthood and pregnancy
2 Physical development
3 Nutrition and health
4 Intellectual, social and emotional development
5 The family and the community
6 Exam questions
7 Internal assessment

The first five units cover the content requirements of the specification, Unit 6 contains practice exam questions and Unit 7 gives you some help and guidance on how to tackle your individual and resource tasks.

Units 1 to 5 cover the topics on double-page spreads, which include the following features.

+ For further reference – these boxes provide extra information that you may wish to explore in more depth, often using the Internet.
+ Link – these features signpost where content in one unit is linked to content in another unit.
+ Key points – these boxes give you a summary of the key learning points throughout a unit and will help you with revision.
+ Key tasks – to test knowledge and understanding.
+ Further work – to give you the opportunity to plan and carry out investigations and tasks, often using ICT. Some of these are coded RT, which means they could be used as a resource task. Others are coded IT, meaning they could be used as starting points for individual tasks.

The teacher's resource file

This book is supported by a teacher's resource file, which provides more information on certain topics, proformas for coursework, resource sheets for use in coursework and examination advice. Your teacher will let you have the sheets you need.

Pre-conceptual care

When considering starting a family, it is important that both partners are ready to take on the responsibilities of providing for and bringing up a baby and that they both really want a baby.

Couples should consider the following factors:

+ maturity
+ financial support
+ accommodation
+ changing lifestyles.

Couples should consider several factors before starting a family

Maturity

Couples need to be mature enough to cope with parenthood and to be able to make decisions together over matters such as discipline and education.

Discussing such issues that may arise when bringing up children, before birth, will prepare future parents for the demands ahead of them.

Financial support

If the couple are to maintain an adequate standard of living, finances need to be planned in advance. If both partners work, one partner may decide to leave their job or, if both are to continue working, the cost of child care must be considered. Essential equipment, for example a cot and clothing, must also be taken into account, as well as the cost of feeding and providing for a growing child.

Link: *For more information on preparing for the needs of a baby see pages 28–31.*

Accommodation

A child needs to be provided with a clean, safe environment within a warm and secure home. The accommodation should be suitable for a baby and be adequate to cope with a growing family. There should be somewhere for a baby to sleep and, as the child grows, space to play (e.g. a garden) and a place where the child can keep his or her possessions (e.g. a bedroom). Facilities that are close by should also be considered, such as parks and pre-school groups.

Changing lifestyles

Couples need to consider the role each of them will take after the birth of the baby. Parents and carers should be aware that their lifestyles will change considerably once the baby has arrived. Here are some factors:

+ one partner may take a career break
+ there will be less money available
+ there will be a loss of freedom
+ babies need 24-hour care
+ having a baby means long-lasting responsibilities.

Providing that all factors are taken into account and children are planned for in a thoughtful and caring manner, they can bring a great deal of pleasure, love, satisfaction and new interests for both partners.

Choosing when to have a baby

With the wide variety of methods of **contraception** available, couples can choose when to begin a family and how many children they would like. Some couples decide not to start a family until they are older.

Link: *For more information on contraception see pages 14–17.*

There are several advantages for planning a family. Parents are:

+ ready to accept the responsibilities of parenthood
+ able to space the arrival of each child

+ able to provide for each child's physical, social, emotional and intellectual needs
+ in a stable, mature relationship.

Pre-conceptual care

Once a couple have made the decision to have a baby, the care of the mother-to-be's health before conception must be considered. This is called **pre-conceptual care**. The main factors to consider are:

+ a good, nutritious diet
+ not to be overweight
+ to be as healthy as possible
+ to give up smoking and drinking alcohol
+ to avoid taking drugs and medicines which may be harmful
+ to check with her GP (doctor) if she is immune to rubella (German measles)
+ to have **genetic counselling** if there is concern about hereditary diseases.

Folic acid should be taken by a woman who hopes to become pregnant and during the early months of the pregnancy. It is one of the B vitamins and it helps to prevent defects such as **spina bifida**. This is an abnormality caused by the brain and spinal cord failing to develop properly. Good sources of folic acid are foods such as nuts, broccoli, whole grain cereals and wholemeal bread. Folic acid supplements can also be taken and are widely available.

Folic acid is found in these foods

Fathers-to-be can support and encourage their partners by also following a healthy diet and giving up smoking and drinking alcohol. All these factors will help to ensure that the baby will be as healthy as possible.

Genetic counselling

Many couples who are planning for a baby may require genetic counselling to seek advice on the risk of disease being passed on from parents to children.

Children inherit **genes** from their parents and these genes contain information such as hair and eye colour, body shape, blood group, etc. They also contain information about any disease which may be inherited by the baby.

Tests can be carried out on the unborn baby to detect any genetic abnormality and, if an abnormality is found, the parents may consider terminating the pregnancy (**abortion**).

Inherited diseases

Some diseases are caused by faulty genes which can be passed down to generations of the same family. Here are some possible diseases:

+ cystic fibrosis – thick mucus blocks the lungs
+ haemophilia – the blood fails to clot
+ thalassaemia – a type of anaemia that is a disorder of the red blood cells
+ PKU (phenylketonuria) – the brain becomes damaged causing the child to be mentally handicapped
+ muscular dystrophy – weakens the muscles.

Key points

+ A couple need to consider several factors before deciding to start a family.
+ Contraception allows couples to plan their family and have children when they are ready.
+ Pre-conceptual care is the health of the woman before conception.
+ Genetic counselling is important for some couples who need advice before having a baby.

Key tasks

1 Write brief notes on the four factors that couples should consider before having a baby.
2 Describe the advantages for planning a family.
3 Explain the term 'pre-conceptual care'.
4 What do you understand by the term 'genetic counselling'?

Conception

When a couple have sexual intercourse, the sperm from the father may fertilize an egg from the mother and a baby will be conceived. In order to understand this process, it is important to know about the female and male reproductive systems.

The female reproductive system

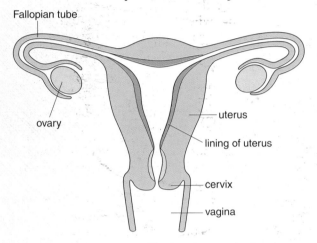

The female reproductive system

The male reproductive system

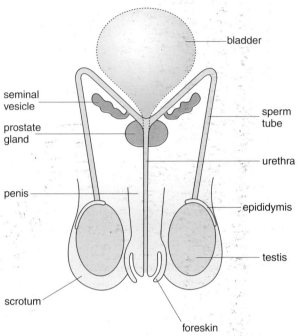

The male reproductive system

Fallopian tube – joins the ovaries to the uterus. Fertilization takes place here

Ovaries – control the female sex **hormones** and produce and release eggs

Uterus – where the baby develops and grows

Lining of the uterus – every month during **menstruation**, this comes away. If an egg is fertilized, it becomes attached to the lining

Cervix – the neck of the uterus that is usually closed

Vagina – during intercourse, sperm are deposited here

Seminal vesicle – stores and secretes **semen**, which carries the sperm

Scrotum – the bag containing the testes

Testis – produce sperm and the male sex hormone

Sperm tube – lead from the testes, and along which the sperm travel

Urethra – a tube which carries semen and urine

Penis – becomes erect before and during intercourse and ejaculates sperm into the vagina

Foreskin – covers and protects the tip of the penis

Epididymis – where the sperm are stored

Menstruation

The average menstrual cycle takes 28 days to complete. The purpose of the cycle is to produce an egg and to prepare the uterus to receive the egg if it is fertilized.

During the first part of the cycle, the lining of the uterus is built up ready to receive an egg. If the egg is not fertilized, the lining of the uterus breaks down and leaves the body in a flow of blood called menstruation or **period**.

Ovulation occurs
around day 14

| 1 | 2 | 3 | 4 | 5 | 6 | 7 | 8 | 9 | 10 | 11 | 12 | 13 | 14 | 15 | 16 | 17 | 18 | 19 | 20 | 21 | 22 | 23 | 24 | 25 | 26 | 27 | 28 |

Menstruation – day 1-5
Lining of the uterus grows – day 6-15
Uterus is ready to receive an egg – day 16-21
Lining of uterus starts to break down – day 22-28

The menstrual cycle

Usually an egg is released every month alternately from one of the ovaries. It is released about halfway through the menstrual cycle on around day fourteen. This process is called **ovulation**. After the egg is released from the ovary, it moves along the Fallopian tube.

Fertilization

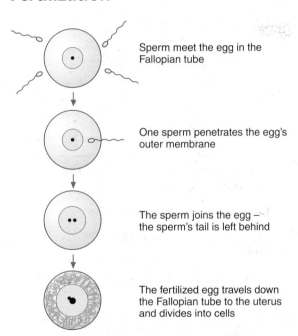

Sperm meet the egg in the Fallopian tube

One sperm penetrates the egg's outer membrane

The sperm joins the egg – the sperm's tail is left behind

The fertilized egg travels down the Fallopian tube to the uterus and divides into cells

How fertilization takes place

Before intercourse, a man's penis becomes erect and it is then able to enter the woman's vagina and ejaculate semen. Semen is a milky substance that contains millions of sperm. From the vagina, the sperm swim into the uterus and along the Fallopian tubes. If an egg has been released from an ovary (ovulation), the sperm may meet an egg in the Fallopian tube. If this occurs, the egg will be fertilized by one of the sperm. **Conception** will have taken place.

The fertilized egg travels down to the uterus. It divides into cells that become attached to the uterus lining, where it will develop and grow into a baby. This is called **implantation**.

Hormones

Hormones play an important part in controlling the menstrual cycle. They act as chemical messengers, travelling through the blood stream and carrying messages to different parts of the body. The hormones from the pituitary gland stimulate the ovaries and the testes to produce the sex hormones. The female sex hormones (**oestrogen** and **progesterone**) are produced by the ovaries. The male sex hormone (**testosterone**) is produced by the testes.

Key points

+ Menstruation occurs on average every 28 days.
+ Ovulation has occurred when an egg has been released from the ovary.
+ Fertilization is when an egg and a sperm join together in the Fallopian tube.
+ Implantation is when the fertilized egg becomes attached to the uterus lining.

Key tasks

1 Describe the functions of the following:
   a Fallopian tube.
   b Ovaries.
   c Uterus.
   d Seminal vesicle.
   e Testis.
   f Sperm tube.
2 Explain what happens during ovulation.
3 Explain the process of fertilization.

The development of the embryo and foetus

Once the fertilized egg is implanted into the uterus lining, it is called the **embryo**. The time between conception and birth is called **pregnancy** and lasts, on average, for 40 weeks from the first day of the last menstrual period.

Development of the embryo

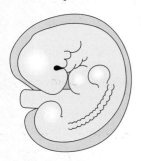

The cells develop very rapidly once implantation has occurred, and these become the embryo. The embryo develops blood, bone and muscles, and the heart starts beating at around three weeks after conception

Development of the foetus

*After eight weeks, the embryo is called the **foetus**. All the main organs of the body are developing and the limbs, hands and feet are forming*

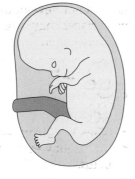

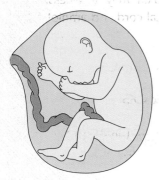

At around 20 weeks, the heartbeat can be heard and the foetus weighs around 350–400g (12–14oz)

*At 28 weeks the foetus is very energetic and kicks freely. The skin is covered in fine, downy hair called **lanugo** and a greasy coating called **vernix**. Vernix protects the skin whilst the baby is in the uterus and is thought to offer some protection against infection after the birth*

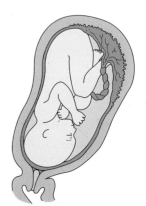

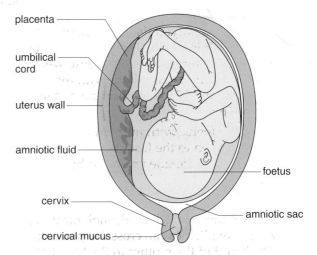

placenta

umbilical cord

uterus wall

amniotic fluid

cervix

cervical mucus

foetus

amniotic sac

At around 40 weeks the foetus is ready to be born. The lanugo will usually have disappeared, but the vernix will remain covering the skin – it is reabsorbed after the birth. The average weight of a baby at birth is approximately 3–3.5kg (7–7.5lbs)

Support and nourishment for the foetus

The fertilized egg not only produces the embryo, it also provides the foetus with the following structures that will support and nourish it until the birth:

+ the **placenta**
+ the **umbilical cord**
+ the **amniotic sac**.

The placenta

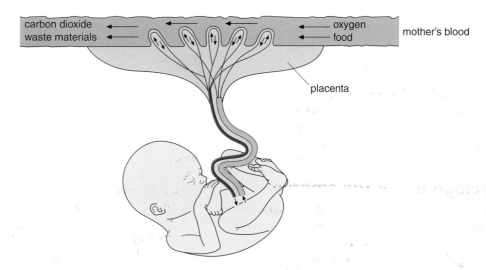

The baby feeds, breathes and excretes wastes through the placenta

The placenta is an organ that is made of soft spongy tissue. It is attached to the wall of the uterus. It is fully formed by the twelfth week and grows steadily to keep pace with the developing foetus. The main functions of the placenta are to:

+ provide the foetus with nutrients
+ provide oxygen to the foetus
+ remove carbon dioxide produced by the foetus
+ excrete waste material.

Harmful substances such as alcohol, nicotine, viruses and medicines can cross the placenta from the blood of the mother to the blood of the foetus. These may damage the developing foetus, especially in the first three to four months of pregnancy.

The umbilical cord

The placenta is linked to the foetus by the umbilical cord, which will grow to be about 50 cm long. The cord contains blood vessels that carry blood to and from the placenta to the foetus.

The amniotic sac

The foetus develops inside the amniotic sac, which is filled with amniotic fluid. The fluid protects the foetus from being damaged and cushions it from any shocks.

Miscarriage

Sometimes, problems can occur in pregnancy and a woman may experience a **miscarriage** – the accidental ending of a pregnancy. Miscarriages most often occur in the twelfth to the fourteenth week and are often the result of the baby or the placenta not developing properly. Subsequent miscarriages may be avoided if the reason for the first can be identified.

Key points

+ Lanugo is fine, downy hair on the foetus's skin.
+ Vernix is a greasy coating covering the skin.
+ After eight weeks, the embryo becomes the foetus.
+ Pregnancy lasts approximately 40 weeks.
+ The placenta, umbilical cord and amniotic sac are the support structures for the foetus.

Key tasks

1 Describe briefly how the embryo and foetus develop up until birth.
2 What are the functions of the placenta?
3 Explain the following terms:
  a Vernix.
  b Umbilical cord.
  c Amniotic sac.

Infertility

The term **infertility** means being unable to conceive and affects up to one in six couples. There are several reasons for infertility and advice can be obtained from a GP (doctor), a family planning clinic, a specialist charity or an infertility clinic. Some couples will need advice and reassurance; others may need drug therapy or surgery.

For further reference

For more information on infertility contact the Human Fertilization and Embryology Authority website at www.hfea.gov.uk

Causes of infertility

If a couple have been trying for a baby for at least two years without success, there are many tests that can be done to find out the reasons why. Possible reasons include:

- a low sperm count in the male – this is when there is a low number of sperm in the semen. A high number of sperm need to be ejaculated at any one time to ensure that conception takes place. Medical conditions, e.g. mumps in boys aged twelve years and over, can cause the sperm count to drop dramatically
- failure to ovulate in the female – this is when the ovaries do not produce eggs. This could be due to hormonal problems or to taking the contraceptive pill for a long time (it often takes time for the menstrual cycle to return to normal, although this is usually only a temporary problem)
- blocked Fallopian tubes – the Fallopian tubes could be blocked, perhaps by an infection, and conception cannot take place
- the cervical mucus in the neck of the uterus may be too thick, preventing the sperm from entering
- the man or woman may have had treatment for cancer that may have left them infertile.

Once tests have established the reason why a couple may be experiencing problems conceiving a baby, advice can be given about any possible treatments. Even after tests, the cause for the infertility may remain unexplained and *in vitro* **fertilization (IVF)** treatment may be suggested to bring the sperm and the eggs together outside the body.

Possible treatments

There are a number of possible treatments available, depending on the reason for the infertility:

- drug therapy to control ovulation if a female is not producing eggs for hormonal reasons. The drugs stimulate egg production and ovulation. This method can cause several eggs to be released together and can result in multiple births, e.g twins
- surgery to improve/repair blocked or damaged Fallopian tubes
- **artificial insemination** using the partner's sperm, or sperm from someone else if the partner has a low sperm count. Artificial insemination involves the injection of sperm into the uterus at the time of ovulation and then fertilization may take place in the usual way. This method may be suitable for those women whose cervical mucus is too thick for sperm to enter the uterus
- *in vitro* fertilization (IVF), where the woman's egg is removed from the ovary and fertilized with the man's sperm in a laboratory. When the embryo is a few days old, it is placed in the woman's uterus and may then develop in the usual way. In order to improve the success of this method, two eggs are fertilized at the same time and returned to the woman's uterus, so this method can result in a multiple birth. This technique is suitable for women with blocked or damaged Fallopian tubes
- **egg donation** with IVF. If a woman cannot produce eggs of her own, another woman donates an egg to be fertilized by the first woman's partner
- **embryo donation**, where the egg of a woman and the sperm of a man are fertilized using IVF and placed in another woman's uterus. This method could be suitable for those couples who cannot produce eggs and who have a low sperm count
- **gamete intra Fallopian transfer (GIFT)** using the couple's own or donated eggs or sperm. GIFT is a method where the eggs and sperm are removed and placed in the Fallopian

tubes to be fertilized. This technique may result in a multiple birth and it is suitable for couples who cannot produce eggs and have a low sperm count, or cannot conceive in the normal way

♦ **intra cytoplasmic sperm injection (ICSI)** is a new technique where a single sperm is injected into an egg in a laboratory. Up to three embryos may be produced, which are then transferred to the uterus in the same way as with IVF. This method is appropriate when the sperm count is low.

Multiple births

Multiple births can happen naturally but some fertility treatments may result in births where there is more than one foetus developing in the uterus. A multiple birth occurs when:

♦ one fertilized egg splits into two parts and develops into two separate individuals, producing **identical twins**. If the split is incomplete, this results in the twins remaining joined together, in the case of **Siamese twins**.

♦ two or more eggs are fertilized by different sperm, producing **non-identical twins**, triplets, quads, quins or sextuplets.

Identical twins

These twins also share the same placenta inside the uterus as they grow and develop. These twins are the same sex and are alike in appearance as they have inherited identical genes.

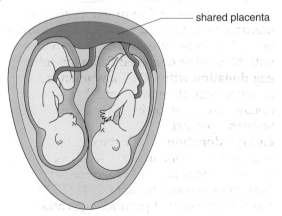

Identical twins share the same placenta

Link: *For more information on pre-conceptual care see pages 6–7.*

Non-identical twins

These develop when two eggs are released at the same time and are both fertilized by different sperm. They have separate placentas.

Non-identical twins can be the same sex, or a boy and a girl. They are no more alike than any other children of the same family.

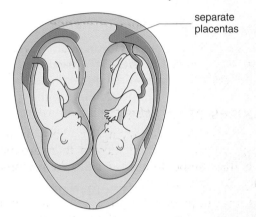

Non-identical twins have their own placenta

Key points

♦ There are many different causes of infertility.
♦ There is a wide variety of possible treatments.

Key tasks

1 List the main causes of infertility.
2 Describe how artificial insemination may result in an egg being fertilized.
3 Explain the following terms:
  a IVF.
  b GIFT.
  c ICSI.
4 Explain how identical twins are formed.

Family planning (1)

Contraception means 'against conception', in other words to prevent having a baby. There are a wide variety of methods of contraception available. Information on contraception can be obtained from a GP or family planning clinic.

Some contraceptives offer protection against **sexually transmitted diseases (STDs)** including **human immunodeficiency virus (HIV)**, which is a virus that can be passed from one person to another during sexual intercourse. A person who is HIV-positive may or may not develop a disease called **AIDS (Acquired Immune Deficiency Syndrome)**. To prevent passing on these diseases, it is important to use the correct method of contraception. In the information that follows, it will be indicated which methods protect against these diseases. These are known as **barrier methods**.

Methods of contraception

Abstention (saying no). 100% effective.

Advantage:

✦ there is no risk of contracting STDs, including HIV.

Male condom – barrier method. 98% effective if used according to instructions. Condoms are made of thin latex (rubber) and fit over the erect penis. They prevent sperm from entering the woman's vagina. A new condom must be used each time.

Female condom (femidom) – barrier method. 95% effective if used according to instructions. Female condoms are made of soft polyurethane (a type of rubber) and line the vagina and the area just outside. They work by stopping sperm from entering the vagina. A new condom must be used each time.

Diaphragm (cap) with spermicide – 92–96% effective if used according to instructions. Diaphragms must be specially fitted by a GP (doctor) to ensure the right size. They are made of flexible rubber or silicone and are used with spermicide (chemicals that kill sperm). Diaphragms cover the cervix and must stay in place for at least six hours after intercourse. Fitting must be checked every twelve months.

Combined pill – Over 99% effective if used according to instructions. The pill is available from family planning clinics and most GPs. It contains two hormones, oestrogen and progestogen, which stop a woman releasing an egg each month (ovulation). Pill users should not smoke.

Progestogen-only pill (POP) – 99% effective if used according to instructions. The POP is available from family planning clinics and most GPs. It contains one hormone, progestogen, which causes changes in the woman's body that make it difficult for sperm to enter the uterus or for the uterus to accept a fertilized egg.

Contraceptive injection – Over 99% effective. The injection releases the hormone progestogen very slowly into the body, preventing a woman from releasing an egg (ovulation). It also thickens cervical mucus to prevent sperm meeting an egg.

Implants – Over 99% effective. A small, flexible tube is placed under the skin of the upper arm, releasing the hormone progestogen into the bloodstream. The implant stops ovulation and prevents the sperm and egg meeting because of the thickening of the cervical mucus.

Key points

✦ Abstention is the only method of contraception that is 100% effective.
✦ The male and female condom are barrier methods.
✦ The combined pill contains two hormones.
✦ The POP contains only one hormone.

Key tasks

1 Name the methods of contraception that may offer protection against STDs.
2 Explain how the following methods offer protection against pregnancy:
   a The combined pill.
   b The progestogen-only pill.
   c The male condom.
   d The diaphragm or cap.

Method of contraception	Advantages	Disadvantages
Male condom 	◆ condoms are available free from family planning clinics and are sold widely in outlets such as supermarkets and chemists ◆ they may protect both partners from STD, including HIV ◆ men can take responsibility for contraception.	◆ putting a condom on can interrupt sexual intercourse ◆ the condom may slip off or split ◆ the man needs to withdraw as quickly as possible after ejaculation.
Female condom (femidom) 	◆ female condoms can be inserted at any time before sexual intercourse ◆ they may protect both partners against STDs, including HIV ◆ they are sold widely and are available free from some family planning clinics.	◆ putting the condom in can interrupt sexual intercourse ◆ they are expensive to buy ◆ you need to make sure the man's penis enters the condom and not between the condom and the vagina.
Diaphragm (cap) with spermicide 	◆ there are a variety of different types to choose from ◆ diaphragms may protect against some STDs and cancer of the cervix ◆ they can be put in any time before sexual intercourse.	◆ putting in a diaphragm can interrupt sexual intercourse ◆ cystitis (bladder infection) can be a problem for some users.
Combined pill 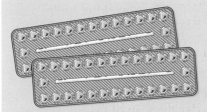	◆ the pill is generally suitable for healthy non-smokers up to the age of the menopause ◆ it protects against cancer of the ovaries, uterus and some pelvic infections ◆ it often reduces period pain, bleeding and pre-menstrual tension.	◆ the pill is not suitable for all women ◆ rare but serious side effects may include blood clots and research suggests an increased risk of cervical and breast cancer ◆ it is not effective if taken more than twelve hours late or after vomiting or severe diarrhoea ◆ some medicines may stop the pill from working.
Progestogen-only pill (POP) 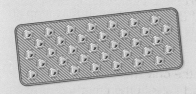	◆ the progestogen-only pill is suitable for older women who smoke ◆ it can be used when breastfeeding.	◆ periods may be irregular ◆ it is less effective in women weighing more than 70kg (11 stones) ◆ it should be taken at the same time each day ◆ it is not effective if taken over three hours late or after vomiting or severe diarrhoea ◆ some medicines may stop the pill from working.
Contraceptive injection 	◆ Depo-Provera – the most commonly used contraceptive injection – protects against pregnancy for twelve weeks ◆ contraception does not have to be thought about ◆ it may protect against cancer of the uterus and some pelvic inflammatory disease.	◆ periods often become irregular ◆ regular periods and fertility may take a year or two to return to normal after stopping the injections ◆ the hormone cannot be removed from the body, so any side effects may continue during the time the injection lasts and some time afterwards ◆ possible side effects may be weight gain, headaches, acne and tender breasts ◆ some prescribed medicines may affect the injection.
Implants 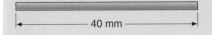 ◄——— 40 mm ———►	◆ a single tube protects against pregnancy for three years; others work for up to five years ◆ contraception does not have to be thought about ◆ once the implant has been removed a woman's fertility returns straight away.	◆ periods are often irregular for the first year ◆ removal of the implant is sometimes difficult ◆ possible side effects include headaches, mood changes and weight gain ◆ some prescribed medicines may affect the implant.

Family planning (2)

Methods of contraception (continued)

Intrauterine device (IUD) – Coil or loop. 98% effective, depending on the type of IUD used. A small plastic and copper device is placed in the uterus by a doctor. It stops sperm meeting an egg or may stop a fertilized egg from implanting in the uterus.

Intrauterine system (IUS) – Over 99% effective. A small plastic device is placed in the uterus by a doctor. The device releases the hormone progestogen, which stops sperm meeting the egg and prevents a fertilized egg from implanting in the uterus. Women are taught to check that the IUS is in place by feeling for the threads high in the vagina.

Female sterilization – Over 99% effective. For female sterilization, the Fallopian tubes are cut, blocked or sealed under general anaesthetic. This prevents the eggs from travelling down the tubes to meet the sperm. Counselling is important to ensure it is the right decision.

Male sterilization (vasectomy) – Over 99% effective. For male sterilization, the tubes carrying the sperm (the vas deferens) are cut under a local anaesthetic. This means that sperm are not present in the semen that is ejaculated. Counselling is important to ensure it is the right decision.

Natural family planning (NFP) – This is knowing how to identify the fertile and infertile times of the menstrual cycle. This will show the times when sexual intercourse can take place when it is unlikely that pregnancy will occur. This method is successful only if both partners are committed to the method.

The NFP method relies on the woman using several natural indicators:

* temperature – the body temperature rises slightly after ovulation. To find out when this happens, the woman's temperature must be taken every morning before getting out of bed and the results recorded on a chart
* cervical secretions – the secretions produced by the cervix change in texture and amount depending on where the woman is in her menstrual cycle

* length of menstrual cycle – this indicator only works if the woman's cycle is very regular i.e. her period starts at the same time each month.

Persona – 94% effective if used according to instructions. Persona is a fertility device available in the UK. It is a hand-held computerized monitor which predicts the fertile and infertile times of the menstrual cycle. Fertility devices work by monitoring changes in temperature, urine and saliva.

Emergency contraception

If intercourse has taken place without using contraception or if a method of contraception has failed, it is possible to use emergency methods.

* Emergency pills (the 'morning after' pill). These must be taken within three days (72 hours) of unprotected sexual intercourse. The pills may delay ovulation or stop a fertilized egg from implanting in the uterus. These pills are mainly provided by doctors on prescription, although they are now available in some chemists without prescription.
* The copper IUD. This is inserted into the uterus (by a doctor) within five days of having unprotected sexual intercourse. It may stop an egg being fertilized or implanting in the uterus.

Key points

+ Male and female sterilization methods are permanent.
+ The IUS releases the hormone progestogen.
+ Emergency contraception is available if other methods have failed.

Key tasks

1 Describe the differences between the IUD and the IUS.
2 Explain the following methods of contraception:
   a Vasectomy.
   b Female sterilization.
3 Explain why natural family planning may be an unreliable method of contraception.

Method of contraception	Advantages	Disadvantages
Intrauterine device (IUD) 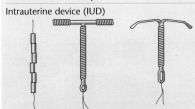	✦ an IUD works as soon as it is inserted ✦ it can stay in place for three to ten years, depending on the type used ✦ contraception does not have to be thought about.	✦ periods may be heavier and longer ✦ an IUD is not suitable for women who already have heavy periods ✦ it is not suitable for women at risk of getting a sexually transmitted disease.
Intrauterine system (IUS) 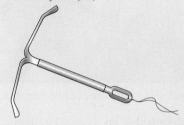	✦ an IUS prevents pregnancy for five years ✦ periods will be lighter and shorter ✦ it works as soon as it is inserted ✦ contraception does not have to be thought about.	✦ irregular light bleeding is likely for the first three months ✦ temporary side effects include breast tenderness and acne.
Female sterilization 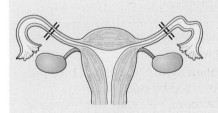	✦ female sterilization is permanent ✦ contraception does not need to be thought about if the operation is successful.	✦ the Fallopian tubes may rejoin ✦ contraception must be used until after the first period after the operation.
Male sterilization (vasectomy) 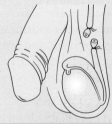	✦ a vasectomy is permanent ✦ contraception does not need to be thought about if the operation is successful.	✦ contraception must be used until there are two negative semen tests (i.e. no sperm is present) ✦ it usually takes a few months for no sperm to be present ✦ the vas deferens may rejoin.
Natural family planning (NFP) 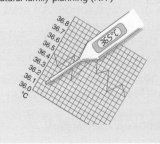	✦ no chemical agents or physical devices are used ✦ there are no side effects ✦ it is acceptable to all faiths and cultures.	✦ it takes between three and six monthly cycles to learn how to use this method effectively, with the guidance of a trained NFP teacher ✦ daily records must be kept ✦ intercourse must be avoided during the fertile time ✦ natural methods do not protect against sexually transmitted diseases.

A healthy pregnancy

Signs of pregnancy

The first sign of pregnancy that a woman may experience is a missed period. Other symptoms may also be noticeable:

+ nausea (known as 'morning sickness' as it often occurs first thing in the morning)
+ tender and enlarged breasts
+ passing urine more frequently
+ darkening of the skin around the nipples
+ constipation.

Health factors to be considered

The mother needs to be aware that there are several factors to consider during the pregnancy to ensure that both the unborn baby and herself are as healthy as possible. These are:

+ eating a healthy diet
+ avoiding certain diseases
+ avoiding certain substances
+ getting a balance of rest and exercise
+ wearing the right clothing.

Link: For more information on nutrition see pages 48–51.

Eating a healthy diet

During pregnancy, it is important to eat a variety of foods to ensure a balanced diet. Foods from the following groups should be chosen on a daily basis:

+ dairy products for calcium, e.g. milk, cheese and yogurt
+ meat, poultry, fish and other protein sources, e.g. eggs, nuts, myco-protein, pulses (peas, beans and lentils)
+ fruit, vegetables and salads for vitamins and minerals. Choose a wide variety, at least five servings and a glass of fruit juice daily
+ starchy foods for the main source of energy. Choose high fibre varieties to prevent constipation, e.g. wholemeal bread, wholegrain cereals, wholewheat pasta, brown rice, potatoes and naan/pitta bread
+ fats and oils for energy, but only a small amount is needed daily, e.g. margarine, low fat spread and olive oil. If too much fat is eaten it is stored in the body as fat.

Folic acid intake should also be increased, especially in early pregnancy.

A variety of foods should be eaten during pregnancy

Avoid fried and spicy foods as this can cause heartburn. The expectant mother does not need to eat extra fat or carbohydrate as this may cause a weight problem.

Link: For more information on pre-conceptual care see pages 6 and 7.

Lactation

If the mother is going to breastfeed her baby, her diet should be similar to when she was pregnant. Eating sensibly is very important in order to keep healthy. Very often, the mother may find she eats more when breastfeeding and, if this is the case, it is advised that the starchy foods are increased. The amount of calcium is important so at least one pint of milk and some cheese and/or yogurt should be taken daily. Alcohol should be kept to a minimum.

Avoiding certain diseases

Listeriosis is a rare disease and is caused by bacteria which grows in certain foods. An attack of this disease can result in miscarriage, stillbirth or illness in the unborn baby. Avoid eating the following foods during pregnancy:

+ soft cheeses, e.g. Brie and blue-veined cheese
+ cook-chill meals unless they are very hot all the way through
+ meat which is not cooked thoroughly
+ products containing raw eggs (e.g. mayonnaise) which may contain the salmonella bacteria
+ liver and foods containing liver (e.g. paté) should be avoided as liver contains large amounts of Vitamin A which could harm the unborn baby.

A few infectious diseases can cause serious problems if contracted and should be avoided:

+ rubella (German measles) – if rubella is caught in early pregnancy (before sixteen weeks), although the mother may be unaffected it can cause severe abnormalities in the unborn baby, i.e. deafness, blindness, heart disease and brain damage
+ chickenpox – pregnant women are advised to avoid children with chickenpox and adults with shingles. If contracted during pregnancy, the mother may become ill and the unborn baby may be affected
+ toxoplasmosis – this disease is usually unnoticed in the mother, but if passed on to the unborn baby it may cause serious problems. It can be passed on by contact with cats' faeces, therefore pregnant women are advised to avoid cat litter trays.

Avoiding certain substances

There are some substances that can cause deformity in the developing baby and should be avoided by the expectant mother:

+ medicines – many medicines are harmful to the unborn baby and should only be taken under the advice of a doctor
+ drugs – this usually refers to those which affect the mind and are habit-forming, e.g. LSD, crack, cannabis and heroin. The baby may be born addicted to the drug
+ alcohol – recent research suggests that alcohol can be taken during pregnancy, but no more than one or two drinks once or twice a week. Regular drinking can interfere with the baby's development and this should be avoided. Many women give up alcohol
+ smoking – smoking can give rise to smaller babies at birth, who are more vulnerable to illness. Heavy smokers are more likely to miscarry or to have a stillborn baby. The chemicals in the smoke can increase the baby's heart-rate so it does not receive as much oxygen in the blood and will not grow as well as those developing in a non-smoker
+ aromatherapy/essential oils – they may cause miscarriage.

A balance of rest and exercise

Exercise is recommended for everyone and that includes the expectant mother. It will ensure that she keeps in good health, and activities such as swimming, walking and cycling are particularly beneficial providing they are done in moderation. Exercise should be balanced with rest, and towards the end of pregnancy a rest during the day will also be beneficial.

Wearing the right clothing

During pregnancy, clothing needs change for obvious reasons. The expectant mother's breasts enlarge and the **abdomen** expands. Therefore, clothing needs to be loose and expandable. Supportive bras are important, as well as comfortable footwear with low heels. This type of footwear will help prevent backache.

A selection of maternity clothing

Key points

+ A healthy lifestyle for the expectant mother is important to ensure her unborn baby is as healthy as possible.
+ Eating a balanced diet, avoiding diseases and certain substances should help her maintain a healthy lifestyle.

Key tasks

1 Describe the type of diet an expectant mother should follow.
2 Explain the diseases that should be avoided by an expectant mother.
3 What effects does smoking have on the unborn baby?

Further work	Prepare a healthy midday meal for an expectant mother. Record the nutritional value of the meal. (RT)

Antenatal provision (1)

Antenatal ('before birth') care is provided during pregnancy and is carried out either by an antenatal clinic, a family doctor (GP) or a community midwife. Regular check-ups and tests are carried out to ensure that the baby is developing normally and that the pregnancy is going well. The first antenatal check-up takes place around weeks eight to ten of pregnancy. Checks are then carried out every month until week 30, when more checks are required.

Routine tests

There are a number routine of tests that are carried out at every visit:

- The mother's weight. On average a pregnant woman puts on about 12kg (2 stones) during pregnancy. If too much weight is gained, she may be advised to adjust her diet.
- Blood pressure. It is important that the mother's blood pressure does not get too high as this may lead to pregnancy-induced hypertension (also called pre-eclampsia), which can be harmful to both mother and baby and may cause premature labour. Other symptoms include swollen ankles and gaining too much weight.

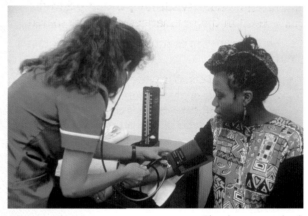

Blood pressure check

- Examination of the uterus. The uterus is examined by the doctor or midwife, who feels the outside of the abdomen to give some idea of the baby's size and position.
- Urine. This is tested for the following:
  - ✦ sugar – if present, it may indicate diabetes in the mother
  - ✦ protein – if present, it may indicate an infection of the kidneys or bladder.

Other tests

A small sample of blood is taken from the mother for a variety of tests at the first visit.

- The mother's blood group, in case she needs a blood transfusion at any time.
- The mother's Rhesus factor. People with the factor are called Rhesus positive and those without the factor are called Rhesus negative. If the mother's blood is Rhesus negative, problems may arise if the baby's father is Rhesus positive. If the baby is Rhesus negative, there is no problem. If the baby is Rhesus positive, the first baby will be all right, but the next Rhesus positive baby could have anaemia, jaundice or developmental problems. Rhesus negative mothers will have their blood tested on giving birth and may need an injection to protect their next baby.
- If the mother is immune to rubella (German measles).
- If the mother has anaemia, to establish if her iron levels are appropriate. If iron levels are low she may need an iron supplement.
- If the mother has syphilis, to detect and treat it. Syphilis can infect the baby.
- If the mother has Hepatitis B, a virus that causes liver disease and may infect the baby if the mother is a carrier or is infected during pregnancy. The baby can be **immunized** at birth to prevent infection.

There are also tests available for Hepatitis C and HIV but these are not routine at present. They are offered if the mother is at risk from either of these viruses. Both of the tests can be done from the same blood sample. Other tests are available for those at risk of thalassaemia (a red blood cell disorder) and sickle cell anaemia (where the red blood cells change shape and there is a shortage of them).

Foetal heartbeat

During the last four months of pregnancy, the foetal heartbeat can be heard through a stethoscope placed on the mother's abdomen.

Ultrasound scan

Ultrasound scans are usually carried out at around weeks twelve and nineteen of pregnancy.

Ultrasound is used to produce pictures of the baby in the uterus. The first scan provides the following information: the baby's age, position, size, position of the placenta, the baby's heartbeat and if there is a multiple pregnancy (more than one baby). The second scan is used to check that the baby is developing normally and it may identify some abnormalities.

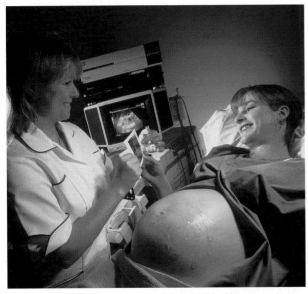

Ultrasound scan

Down's risk screening test

The Down's test is used to find out the risk of having a baby with **Down's syndrome**. A blood sample is taken between fourteen and twenty weeks of pregnancy and the result is available within two weeks. If the mother falls into the high risk group following this test, further tests – such as **amniocentesis** – may be necessary.

AFP test

Using the same blood sample, another test is also available, called the **Alphafetoprotein (AFP) test**. This test is for screening spina bifida and can be offered to the mother independently from the Down's test if she prefers not to be screened for Down's. Some mothers may decide not to have the AFP test if they are against **terminating** the baby.

Amniocentesis

This test is used to detect Down's syndrome and is usually carried out from fifteen weeks onwards. An ultrasound scan is carried out and

a hollow needle is inserted through the abdominal wall into the uterus. Some of the amniotic fluid is removed using the needle. There is a risk of miscarriage with this test, and the results take about two to three weeks. There are several reasons for having an amniocentesis:

- the Down's risk screening test has shown a high risk for Down's syndrome
- the mother is older than average, which could increase the risk of Down's syndrome
- the family has a history of inherited chromosome or health problems.

CVS test

The **chorionic villus sampling (CVS)** test involves removing a small sample of placenta tissue during an ultrasound scan, using a hollow needle which is passed through the abdominal wall into the uterus. It is carried out after ten weeks of pregnancy and can detect Down's syndrome. There is a risk of miscarriage with this test, but results may be available within three to four days, which is much sooner than the amniocentesis. The mother has the option of an early termination if the result is abnormal. This test is offered to those mothers who are older or who have a family history of inherited chromosome and health problems.

The amniocentesis and CVS tests are used for detecting Down's syndrome, and, if positive, may result in the pregnancy being terminated.

Key points

- ✦ An antenatal clinic is where mothers-to-be go for regular testing to ensure they are as well as possible and the baby is developing normally.
- ✦ Amniocentesis and CVS are both tests which can detect Down's syndrome.

Key tasks

1 Describe the following antenatal tests:
   a Blood pressure.
   b Weight.
   c Urine.
2 What is the purpose of the first blood test?
3 Why is an ultrasound scan carried out?
4 Describe the amniocentesis test.

Antenatal provision (2)

Antenatal classes

As well as attending an antenatal clinic for regular tests, the expectant mother will be advised to attend antenatal classes. In these classes, mothers learn about the following things:

+ the development of the unborn baby
+ how to maintain a healthy lifestyle in pregnancy
+ methods of pain relief available during the birth
+ relaxation and breathing exercises
+ breast and bottle feeding
+ how to handle and care for the new baby.

Expectant mothers and fathers at antenatal classes

Antenatal classes provide the opportunity for the father-to-be to attend, so that he can help and support his partner. He will learn about pregnancy and how to help during the birth, so he will be prepared, will know what to expect and can give encouragement to the mother. Both mother and father will be able to ask any questions and meet other expectant parents.

Methods of delivery

Most babies are born in hospital, but there are also a number who are born at home. Whether a baby is born at home or hospital, it is important that both mother and baby receive the best possible care to ensure a safe delivery.

There are a variety of reasons why some mothers are advised to have their baby in hospital. These include:

+ those having their first baby
+ those who have experienced previous problems during birth
+ those who have a history of miscarriage or other pregnancy complications, e.g. diabetes
+ those who are over the age of 35
+ those having a multiple birth
+ those living in poor home conditions, as this may be a health risk to both mother and baby.

These mothers are advised to have their babies in hospital in order to provide them with the best possible facilities in case a complication arises during the birth.

Those mothers who do not meet any of the above criteria may have a choice where to have their baby. They should consider the following information about hospital and home delivery.

Hospital delivery

Advantages:

+ the mother will have the opportunity to talk to other mothers
+ she will be free from household responsibilities, and should have the chance to rest and relax whilst the baby is asleep
+ special equipment is available should an emergency occur
+ the mother's and baby's health can be monitored throughout labour.

Disadvantages:

+ the mother will have little privacy
+ she will not know the midwife who is looking after her
+ she may be in unfamiliar surroundings
+ visitors will be restricted to visiting times.

Some mothers who have their baby delivered normally may stay in hospital for only about six hours after the birth. They will then go home, where the community midwife takes care of both the baby and the mother.

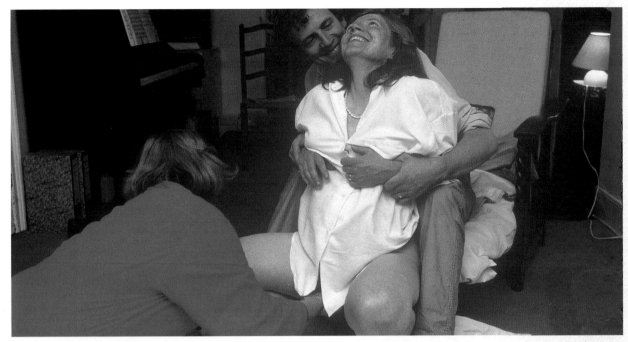

A home delivery

Home delivery

Advantages:

- the mother will have more choice when giving birth to her baby at home
- she may have all her family present at the birth
- she will know the midwife and doctor who are looking after her
- she will not be restricted to hospital routines
- she will be able to take care of the baby in her own way.

Disadvantages:

- the mother will not have so much rest as there may be household responsibilities and other children to look after
- she will not have the contact with other mothers
- if a problem occurs during the birth, the mother may need to be taken to hospital
- there may be a lack of specialist monitoring equipment.

Key points

- ✦ An antenatal class is where expectant mothers find out about looking after their baby and what to expect during labour.
- ✦ Fathers-to-be may also attend antenatal classes in order to know how to support their partner during labour.
- ✦ Hospital deliveries are more common than home deliveries because many women are advised not to give birth to their baby at home.

Key tasks

1 Suggest six pieces of information that may be provided at an antenatal class.
2 Suggest four reasons why a mother may be advised not to have her baby delivered at home.
3 Discuss the advantages and disadvantages of a home versus a hospital delivery.

Further work

Carry out a survey amongst expectant mothers to investigate the antenatal facilities in your area. Record your findings. (RT)

Birth (1)

At around 40 weeks after conception, the baby is ready to be born. The process of giving birth is called **labour**.

There are three signs that indicate to the mother that labour has started. She may experience one or more of the following:

✦ a **show** – a plug of mucus mixed with blood may come away from the cervix (neck of the uterus), indicating that it is beginning to open

✦ the **breaking of the waters** – the amniotic sac containing the amniotic fluid in which the baby has been developing may break, releasing the fluid

✦ **contractions** begin – these usually start slowly (every 20 to 30 minutes) and become stronger and more frequent during the first stage of labour (see below).

The onset of labour is usually slow, allowing the mother time to prepare for the birth. Labour is divided into three stages.

Stage 1

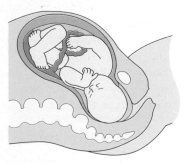

Baby in the first stage of labour

The contractions of the muscles of the uterus wall gradually open the cervix until it is wide enough for the baby's head to pass through (it is fully dialated when it measures 10cm in diameter). Towards the end of the first stage the contractions may be every two minutes. The first stage is the longest, and for a first baby, can last up to twelve to eighteen hours on average.

There are several methods of pain relief which can be used to help the mother through labour and these are discussed on pages 26 to 27.

If possible, it is easier for the mother if she can walk about during the early part of this stage. During the latter part of this stage each mother will find a position that suits her, for example lying on her side or kneeling on all fours.

Stage 2

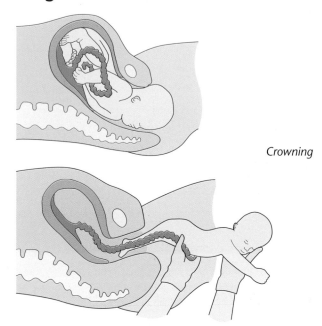

Crowning

Stage 2 is now complete

The cervix will now be fully dilated and the uterus, cervix and vagina have become the **birth canal**. Contractions are very strong and push the baby along the birth canal. The midwife will indicate to the mother when to start pushing and the baby's head will be pushed out from the vagina. This process is called **crowning**. The midwife will then ease the shoulders out and the baby will be born.

Occasionally the vagina does not stretch sufficiently to allow the baby's head to pass out. When this happens, a small cut is needed to widen the opening. This is called an **episiotomy**. The cut is then stitched together after the birth.

Stage 3

After the birth, the umbilical cord is clamped in two places and a cut is made between them. The baby is now a separate person. The contractions continue until the placenta (or **afterbirth**) is delivered through the vagina. Labour is now completed. The baby is carefully examined at birth and is given to the mother to hold as soon as possible.

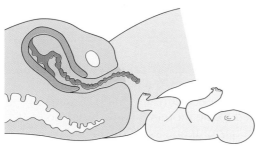

The cord is clamped and cut

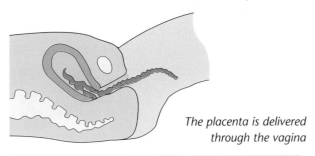

The placenta is delivered through the vagina

Link: For more information on postnatal examination see pages 32–33.

Complications during birth

Sometimes complications occur during the birth and special treatment may be required in order to deliver the baby.

✦ **Breech birth**. Babies are usually born head first, but occasionally they are born either feet or bottom first. This is called the breech position.

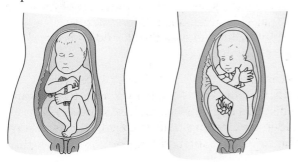

Breech births are either legs first (left) or bottom first (right)

✦ **Forceps delivery**. Forceps may be needed if the baby is in an awkward position or if the mother is becoming exhausted and

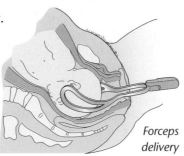

Forceps delivery

the contractions are not strong enough to push the baby out. The baby may need to be eased out of the birth canal with forceps. These are metal instruments that fit around the baby's head and help to ease it out.

✦ **Ventouse** (suction) delivery. A special cap is connected to a suction pump. The cap is then placed against the head of the baby and a vacuum is created. The doctor or midwife pulls on this until the baby is born.

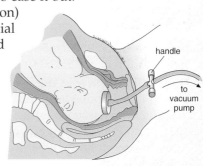

Ventouse delivery

✦ **Caesarian section**. This involves an operation to remove the baby. An incision is made through the abdominal wall of the uterus so the baby can be removed. A caesarian can be carried out under general anaesthetic or using an epidural anaesthetic so that the mother may remain conscious and the father can be present. Caesarians are performed if the birth canal is too small, if the baby is in the breech position or if the health of the baby or mother makes immediate delivery necessary.

✦ **Induction**. Sometimes labour needs to be started off artificially. This is called induction. Babies are induced because the baby is overdue by fourteen days or because the baby's or mother's health is at risk. It is possible to induce labour by breaking the waters, or by setting up a hormone drip that signals to the uterus to start contracting.

Key points

✦ The process of giving birth is called labour.
✦ There are three stages of labour.
✦ Some complications in labour may result in babies needing special assistance or treatment in order to be delivered safely.

Key tasks

1 Briefly describe the three stages of labour.
2 What is a Caesarian section and why might it be necessary?
3 Describe the difference between a forceps and a ventouse delivery.

Birth (2)

Pain relief

Labour can be a painful experience for many mothers. There are a number of different types of pain relief available, and these are discussed at antenatal classes.

The midwife will give details on all the options of pain relief available so that the mother can consider which one is best for her. It is a difficult decision to make before going into labour as the mother will not know what the pain is going to be like. It is best to have all the methods explained in advance so she can understand what is involved.

Methods of pain relief

a **Relaxation and breathing exercises**. These are natural childbirth techniques that help to relieve the pain without the aid of any pain killers. These are taught in antenatal classes.

b **Entonox**. This is a mixture of nitrous oxide and oxygen which is breathed through a mask or mouthpiece. It does not harm the baby, but acts quickly and wears off in minutes. Entonox can be used at any time during labour when the mother feels it is necessary, but it may make her feel a little sick or light-headed.

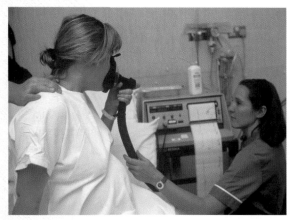

Entonox (sometimes known as 'gas' or 'gas and air') is made up of 50 per cent nitrous oxide and 50 per cent oxygen

c **Pethidine**. This is an injection that can make the mother and the baby feel drowsy, which is why it is only given in the early stages of labour. It may also make the mother feel a little sick.

d **Transcutaneous electrical nerve stimulation (TENS)**. This is when a gentle electrical current is passed through four flat pads attached to the mother's back. It has no known harmful effects on the baby.

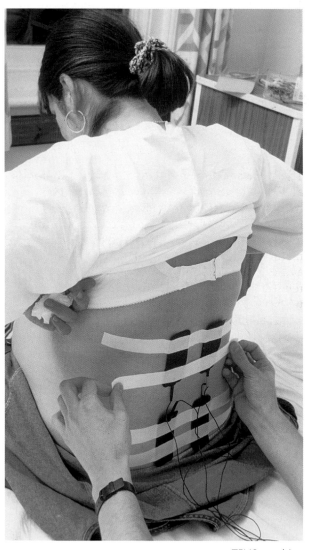

TENS machine

e **Epidural anaesthetic**. This is the most effective method of pain relief and it has little effect on the baby. It is given through a fine tube inserted into the mother's lower back and numbs the mother from the waist downwards. Mobile epidurals are now available – these allow a small amount of movement, e.g. the mother is able to sit in a chair or possibly, with help, to walk to the toilet.

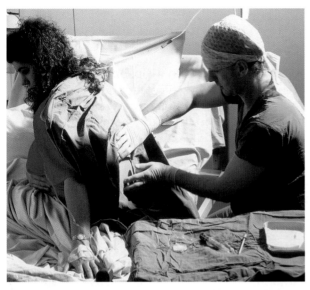

An epidural being administered by an anaethetist

There are a variety of other, alternative methods available in some hospitals that can also be helpful during the early stages of labour. Relaxation is important, and moving around often helps to ease the pain. The following methods may be available in some hospitals, and often the mother can arrange her own pain relief – for example, an aromatherapist to go with her:

+ music and aromatherapy – essential oils are massaged into the skin whilst listening to music
+ homeopathy – these remedies are taken from plants and minerals and are used under the advice of a homeopath
+ acupuncture – tiny needles are inserted into points on the earlobe, which release the body's natural painkillers. Needles are attached to a TENS machine
+ water birth – warm water helps with relaxation and birthing pools can be hired for a home birth

+ reflexology – the massaging of the feet can release the body's natural pain killers.

The father's role

The father's role throughout labour is important to the mother as he can support and encourage her at all times, as well as be present for the birth of his child. It can also be beneficial to the mother to have a familiar person with her in a hospital environment.

Key points

+ Several types of pain relief are available to help the mother during the birth.
+ Some hospitals offer a range of alternative methods of pain relief.
+ The father is encouraged to take part in the birth.

Key tasks

1 Describe the following methods of pain relief:
  a Relaxation and breathing exercises.
  b Entonox.
  c Pethidine.
  d TENS.
  e Epidural anaesthetic.
2 Explain the alternative methods of pain relief.
3 Why is the role of the father important during labour?

Further work

1 Investigate the different methods of pain relief available in your area. Record your results using ICT. (RT)
2 Design and make a leaflet on the methods of pain relief available for the expectant mother. (RT)

Preparing for the baby (1)

It is important for parents and carers to prepare for the physical, social and emotional needs of the new baby to ensure that the baby will be growing within a warm, secure and loving environment.

Social and emotional needs

Parents and carers need to be aware that babies are influenced by the environment they are brought up in from an early age. Cuddling a baby is very important so that the baby will be comforted and will feel secure. The baby needs to develop feelings of affection. In order for this to take place, he or she needs close contact to establish and form emotions towards the people around her or him.

Link: *For more information on emotional development see pages 92–95.*

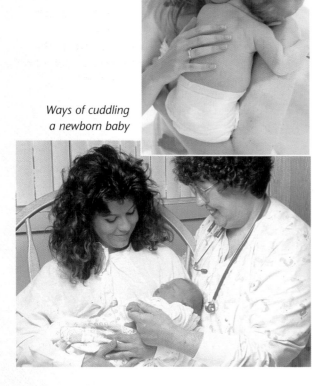

Ways of cuddling a newborn baby

Smiling and talking to the baby is also recognized as being very important for the baby to develop socially. Babies use their eyes and ears to watch and listen to what is going on around them. If the baby is spoken to, she or he will soon respond and interact to that person by smiling and making noises.

Link: *For more information on social development see pages 86–89.*

Providing toys and things to look at will also help the baby to develop physically and intellectually. A mobile above the cot, pictures on the wall and music to listen to will encourage development.

Physical needs

Physically, a baby requires both clothing and certain items of nursery equipment. Some of the nursery items allow the baby to react socially and emotionally with family members and others who are around the baby – for example, a high chair at mealtimes allows social interaction to take place.

The first set of baby clothes is often called the **layette**. Many mothers-to-be enjoy collecting and buying articles of clothing, but a new baby requires only a few. There are some points to consider when buying clothing for a baby. They should be:

+ soft
+ warm
+ loose and comfortable
+ washable
+ non-irritant (will not irritate the skin)
+ flame resistant (will not catch fire easily)
+ easy to put on and take off.

Here are some examples of items that may be necessary:

+ vests – these are worn next to the skin and made of soft fabric
+ stretch suits – all-in-one and enclose the feet
+ cardigans – used when an extra layer is needed for warmth
+ hat – needed for hot and cold weather
+ shawl – warm and lightweight
+ socks – to keep the feet warm
+ bootees/padders – to keep the feet warm

- sleep suits – needed for warmth on cold nights and made of fleecy fabric
- pram suits – padded, all-in-one suits for outdoor wear.

Nappies also need to be purchased for the new arrival. There are three different types:

- terry nappies – these are made of terry towelling, which is a hard-wearing, absorbent material. Terries are expensive to buy but, once bought, can be used again and again and should last for at least one baby.
- disposable nappies – these are available in different sizes and are unisex (meaning suitable for a boy or a girl). They save time as they are thrown away instead of being washed, but they are more expensive in the long term. Disposable nappies are non-biological, which means they do not rot down, and therefore are a possible threat to the environment.
- reusable nappies – these are becoming more popular and are washable nappies that can be used more than once. They are made of flannelette, have adjustable waistbands, elasticated leg openings and lined with absorbent pads.

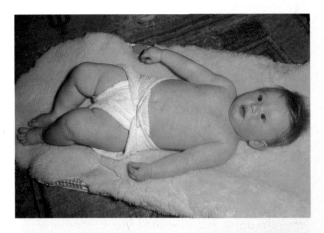

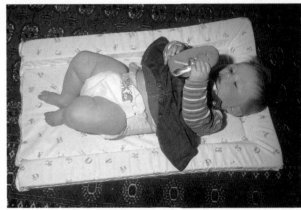

Babies in a terry and a disposable nappy

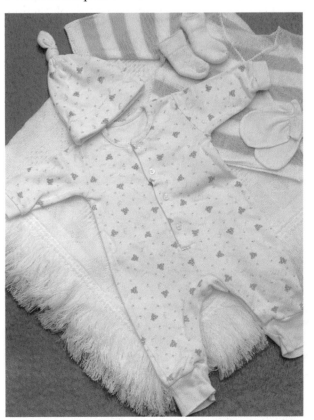

Items for a layette

Key points

- ✦ Parents and carers need to be prepared for the arrival of the new baby so that they can provide the appropriate environment.
- ✦ Parents and carers should be aware that the way they behave and react towards their new baby will influence how the baby develops.

Key tasks

1 Suggest six points to consider when choosing clothing for a new baby.
2 Compare the differences between disposable and terry nappies.
3 Explain how parents and carers can help a newborn baby to develop socially and emotionally in the early days.

Further work Carry out a survey into the babycare products that are available to help keep a baby clean. Use ICT to record your findings. (RT)

Preparing for the baby (2)

As well as clothing, a baby will need several pieces of equipment to sleep, sit and play in. There is a wide variety of equipment available, some essential and some non-essential, depending on the expectant couple's lifestyle. The parents and carers need to choose wisely and to buy items that suit their finances. All nursery equipment should carry a kitemark. This is a safety label that shows the equipment has been made to the correct British Standard.

Prams

Prams are available in various styles. Some can be converted into a carrycot and pushchair – these are the most versatile and economical. Whatever style of pram is bought, it should:

+ be sturdy and strong
+ have safe brakes
+ be weather resistant
+ be well balanced and easy to steer.

Pushchairs and buggies

These are generally used for the older baby or child. A wide variety of pushchairs and buggies are available and these are generally easier for shopping and travelling than a pram. Pushchairs fold for easy storage and may have various features, e.g. a shopping basket, hood and apron for protection against the weather. All pushchairs should be fitted with a safety harness for the baby/child to be held in safely.

Baby carriers

Slings and baby carriers are a convenient method of transporting a young baby or older child when pushchairs or prams are impractical.

Cot

Cots are a useful piece of equipment for the baby to sleep in. Parents and carers should consider the following points before purchasing a cot:

+ the bars must be no more than 6 cm apart
+ it should have a well fitting waterproof mattress with no gaps anywhere.

Carrycots/moses baskets

These can be used for newborn babies and ensure a warm, snug environment for sleeping.

Travel cots

Travel cots are useful items if travelling on holiday or visiting relatives and friends. Some can also be used as a playpen for when the baby is mobile.

Blankets and sheets

Blankets and sheets should be easy to wash and lightweight. Pillows and duvets should never be used with babies under the age of one year, as there may be a risk of suffocation in a young baby.

Walking reins

Walking reins with a safety harness are essential for toddlers, as they can experience walking skills while remaining under the control of an adult.

Bouncing cradle

A bouncing cradle is useful for the baby to sit in and take notice of the surroundings. This should not be placed on a high surface, as the chair may fall off.

High chair

A high chair is useful so that the older baby (from about six months) can sit at the table with the rest of the family and join in at mealtimes. Some high chairs will convert into a low chair. A safety harness should be used in both styles of chair.

Car seats

Car seats are essential when the baby is going to be travelling in the car.

Link: For more information on car seats see page 119.

Baby baths, playpens and baby bouncers can also be bought, and, although these are not essential items, many parents and carers find them useful.

Key points

+ A selection of clothing and equipment will need to be purchased but care should be taken not to overspend if on a budget.
+ Some items of nursery equipment are non-essential but it is up to the parents and carers whether these are purchased.

Key tasks

1 What points should parents or carers consider when buying the following items of equipment?
   a A pram.
   b A cot.
2 What are the advantages of buying the following pieces of equipment?
   a A travel cot.
   b A bouncing cradle.
   c Walking reins.
   d A high chair.
   e A pushchair/buggie.

Further work	Investigate the most popular items of nursery equipment and record the cost of these items using ICT. (RT)

▼ Carrycots/moses baskets

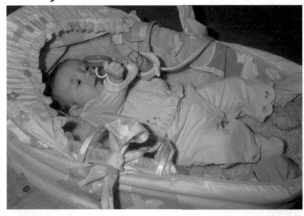

▼ Prams

▼ High chair

▼ Bouncing cradle

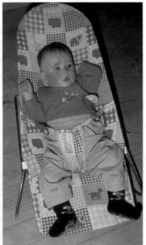

▼ Walking reins

▼ Pushchairs and buggies

▼ Baby carriers

Travel cots

▼ Cot

Postnatal provision

The term **postnatal** refers to the days and weeks immediately following the birth of a baby. There are two professionals who look after, advise and support the mother and newborn baby.

The midwife

The midwife will visit every day until the baby is at least ten days old. If the mother is still in hospital, the midwives there will offer support. If the mother is at home, the community midwife will visit on a daily basis. Both mother and baby are checked at every visit to ensure they are progressing well.

The health visitor

A mother having a visit from the health visitor

The health visitor will take over from the midwife after about ten days and will visit for usually up to six weeks after that. Alternatively, the mother may see the health visitor at the baby clinic, which is usually held on the same day each week at the nearest health centre. Health visitors:

+ provide support and promote good health for both baby and mother

+ answer any questions and concerns
+ advise on immunizations
+ weigh the baby regularly to check progress
+ keep checks on the baby's developmental progress
+ provide opportunities to meet and share experiences with other new mothers.

> Link: *For more information on immunizations see pages 68–69.*

Examination of the baby

The day following the birth, the baby will be examined by a doctor. The doctor:

+ checks the baby's eyes
+ listens to the heart
+ checks the number of fingers and toes
+ checks the mouth for a cleft palate – this is where the roof of the mouth has not formed properly and a small operation will be required
+ checks for congenital dislocation of the hip – the hip joints are tested for movement and treatment is necessary if the hip is dislocated to prevent permanent damage.

> Link: *For more information on physical disabilities see page 110.*

The neo-natal screening test

This involves taking a sample of blood from the baby at around the sixth day after the birth. The baby's heel is pricked to collect the sample and this is tested for three conditions:

a Phenylketonuria (PKU). This is a rare disorder that is caused by an enzyme deficiency which makes the baby unable to use an acid present in milk and other foods. If left untreated, PKU can affect the baby's mental development and he or she could become mentally handicapped. Treatment involves putting the baby on a special diet.
b Congenital hypothyroidism. The thyroid gland (situated just below the voice box) may be missing or not functioning correctly. This slows down physical and mental development, resulting in children being undersized and having learning difficulties.

Treatment involves taking the thyroid hormone, thyroxine.

c Cystic fibrosis. This is a disorder that gives rise to chronic lung disease. There is no complete cure as yet, but if early treatment can be given the child can be helped to grow up physically stronger.

Umbilical cord

The stump of the umbilical cord dries, shrivels and drops off within seven to ten days following the birth.

Vitamin K

It is recommended that all babies are given an injection of Vitamin K within the first 24 hours of birth. Vitamin K is essential in the blood clotting process.

The mother

At around six weeks after the birth, the mother has a postnatal examination. This is carried out by either the hospital or the family doctor. The mother is examined to ensure she is healthy and that her uterus has returned to normal. The baby is also examined to make sure normal progress is being made.

The mother is encouraged to carry out gentle postnatal exercises to help tighten the abdominal muscles and the muscles of the pelvic floor (those muscles in the groin that can be controlled when passing urine and which have been stretched during pregnancy and birth).

Postnatal depression

In the week following the birth, it is common for the mother to feel down and depressed. This is known as the 'baby blues' and, with support and help from family and midwives, these feelings should pass within a few days. Reasons for the 'baby blues' may include:

+ lack of sleep because of disturbed nights
+ hormonal changes
+ the mother feeling she has no time for herself.

However, if these feelings develop into long-term depression this is more serious, and requires advice and help from the doctor.

The father

The father's role immediately after the birth is very important in supporting the mother, helping with household tasks and sharing the care of the baby. It is possible for him to obtain paternity leave (time off from work) of up to two weeks.

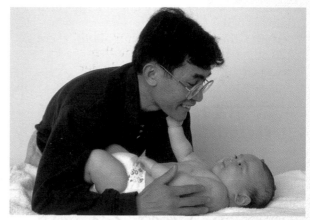

A father bonding with his baby

Registration of the birth

The baby needs to be registered by the parents within six weeks of the birth. The child's name must be given to the Registrar before a birth certificate can be issued.

Key points

+ The midwife is responsible for the welfare of the mother and baby for the first ten days after the birth.
+ The health visitor then takes over and is responsible for the baby's developmental progress and well-being.
+ The mother is required to have a postnatal examination six weeks after the birth to ensure she is healthy.
+ The father's support is invaluable at this time.

Key tasks

1 Describe the role of the health visitor.
2 Explain the neo-natal screening test.
3 What do you understand by the term 'postnatal depression'?

The newborn baby

'Neo-natal' is the term used for the first week after the birth. When a baby is born, body measurements are taken straight afterwards. The three measurements normally recorded are:

+ weight – the average weight of a full-term baby is 3.5kg (7.5lbs)
+ length – the average length is about 50 cm (20 inches)
+ head circumference – the average measurement around the head is about 35 cm (13.5 inches).

Characteristics of a newborn baby

The colour and amount of hair on a newborn baby varies. Some have hardly any hair, others have a large amount. Babies can see when they are born, but they are short-sighted. Fingernails and toenails are present at birth. The head is more developed than the body and is big compared to the rest of the body. On top of the head is a 'soft spot' called the **fontanelle**. This is where the four bones that make up part of the skull have not yet joined together. It will take twelve to eighteen months for the bones to fuse.

At birth the baby's skin is covered in a greasy, white substance called **vernix**.

Link: For more information on vernix see pages 10–11.

A number of babies develop mild **jaundice** around the second or third day after birth. This causes the skin and eyes to be tinged yellow. This is normal and usually clears up on its own within three or four days without any treatment.

Some babies are born with birthmarks. Many of these may disappear over a period of time, but others may be with the child for life.

Reflex actions

A newborn baby shows several reflex actions. These are movements which are automatic. They are caused by the baby's senses being stimulated. They disappear within three months of birth.

Immediately after birth, a newborn baby is examined by a doctor. The doctor or midwife will test the following reflex actions:

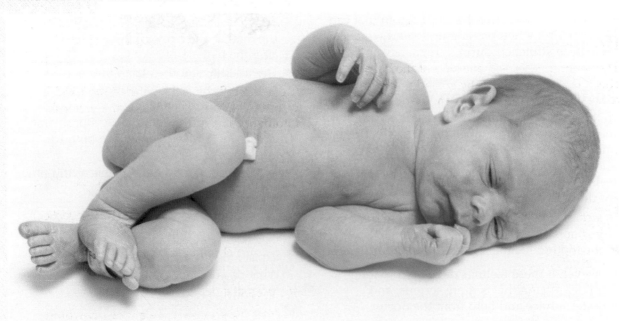

The newborn baby

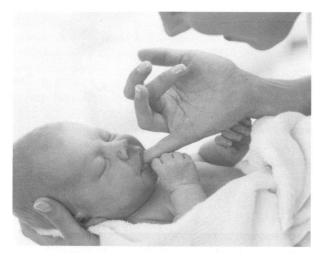

The sucking reflex – a baby will suck on anything that is put into his or her mouth.

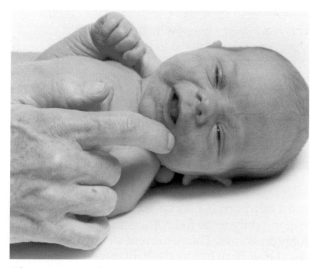

The rooting reflex – if one side of the baby's cheek is touched, the baby's head will turn towards it searching for the mother's nipple.

The stepping reflex – when held upright with the feet on a flat surface, the baby will make forward stepping movements.

The startle reflex – if startled by a sudden loud noise or bright light, the baby will move arms outwards with elbows bent and hands clenched.

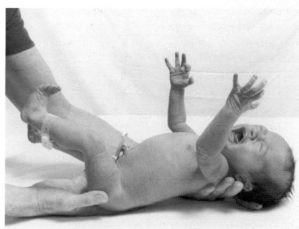

The falling ('Moro') reflex – sudden movements that affect the neck give the baby the feeling that he/she may be dropped, so the baby will fling out the arms and open hands as if falling.

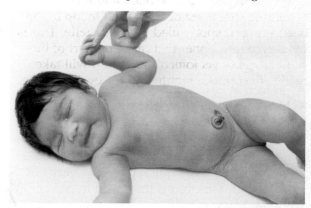

The grasp reflex – if the palm of the hand is touched with an object or finger, the hand automatically grasps it.

Key points

✦ A newborn baby has a 'soft spot' called the fontanelle.
✦ Newborn babies have many characteristics along with reflex actions that all disappear in a relatively short time after birth.

Key tasks

1 What is the average weight of a newborn baby?
2 Describe the fontanelle.
3 List the six reflex actions of a newborn baby.

The needs of a newborn

All new babies have basic needs

All newborn babies have the same basic needs in order to live, grow and develop in the best possible conditions. They need:

+ warmth
+ protection
+ food
+ sleep
+ love
+ security.

Warmth

A newborn baby cannot control its own body temperature so it can quickly become very hot or very cold. This means they need to be kept in constant, warm conditions. The baby's room should be kept at around 20°C (68°F). In an unheated, cold room a baby's body temperature can drop dramatically. On the other hand, a baby can quickly overheat if they have too many layers of clothing or bedding. Parents need to be vigilant and to be aware of the temperature around the baby.

Protection

A newborn baby needs to be protected and kept safe. This means, for example, not leaving a baby outside a shop, even for a minute, in case of unwanted attention from strangers. Babies are vulnerable and cannot protect themselves, so others must do it for them.

Link: *For more information on protection see pages 114–121.*

Food

A baby needs food in the form of milk and may be either breast or bottle fed. Several feeds a day are required.

Link: *For more information on feeding see pages 56–61.*

Sleep

Newborns spend much of their time asleep

Most newborn babies spend a lot of time asleep, waking only to be fed. Others may be awake for longer periods. The pattern of sleep is not regular at first, but as the baby becomes more aware of daylight and everyday noises the pattern becomes more regular.

The position of sleeping is very important. It is advised that babies sleep on their backs until they are old enough to turn over on their own.

A **cot death** (sudden infant death syndrome, or SIDS) is the sudden and unexpected death of a baby for no obvious reason after the baby has been put in the cot to sleep, although it can also happen in a pram, the car or even in someone's arms. In recent years the number of cot deaths has fallen owing to parents and carers following this advice:

+ babies should lie on their backs
+ keep the baby's environment free from tobacco smoke
+ do not let babies overheat
+ breastfeeding helps protect babies against infection

- place the baby with his or her feet at the bottom of the cot to prevent them wriggling under the covers
- if the baby is unwell, seek medical advice.

Cot death can affect babies up to the age of two years, but the majority of cot deaths occur in babies under the age of one year, and happen, without any warning.

Love and security

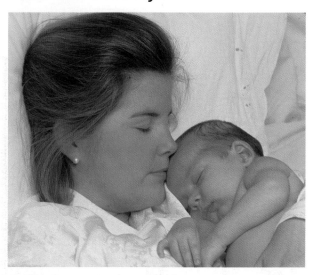

Bonding between mother and baby

Close contact is important for a newborn baby. **Bonding** is the unconditional love between parents and their child. It should develop through close skin and eye contact in the early weeks of life.

Crying

Crying is a baby's way of communicating with others in order to tell them that something is needed. Babies cry for a number of reasons:

- thirst
- sudden noises
- hunger
- discomfort
- tiredness
- boredom
- pain
- loneliness
- dislike of the dark.

Babies cry for several reasons

Whatever the reason for crying, a baby should never be left to cry for too long. Soothing noises using a low voice or playing soft music often calms a baby. Gentle rocking may also soothe a restless baby.

Premature babies

A **premature baby** (pre-term) is one who is born before 37 weeks of pregnancy or a full-term **low birth weight baby** weighing less than 2.5kg (5.5lbs). These babies need special care as they may have problems with:

- breathing
- sucking
- maintaining their own body temperature (keeping warm).

Incubators

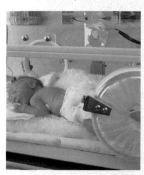

A premature baby is kept in an incubator from birth. An incubator is an apparatus that can be seen through and acts like the uterus for the under-developed baby. The incubator also keeps the baby isolated and offers protection. It provides the baby with:

A premature baby in an incubator

- oxygen to help with breathing problems
- a tube that will supply the baby with food
- constant humidity and temperature control.

Parents and carers are encouraged to play a part in caring for their baby to allow bonding to take place.

Key points

- ✦ The needs of a newborn baby are basic, but very demanding on parents and carers, who will find that caring for a baby is a 24-hour job.
- ✦ Babies who are born prematurely require special care and attention, as well as all the basic needs.

Key tasks

1 What are the basic needs of a newborn baby?
2 Why is it advisable that newborn babies sleep on their backs?
3 Explain the problems that a premature baby may experience and how they can be corrected.

Stages of development (1)

Physical development is the development of the body, and the way the child acquires skills as it progresses. Throughout the sections on development, the term **milestones** will be referred to, as well as the ages of children. Milestones of development are a way of assessing the progress of a baby/child and are used to monitor development.

Developmental screening tests are carried out at regular intervals at a health clinic, GP's surgery or by the health visitor. This involves observing the child in a series of tests.

The ages given are average ages of children, and it is normal for there to be variations in their developmental progress. They are to be used only as a rough guide.

The normal progression of development depends on various factors:

+ the genes the child has inherited
+ the health of the child
+ the environment in which the child is brought up
+ the stimulation and encouragement provided by the parents.

There are two areas of physical development:

a **Gross motor skills**. Gross motor skills involve the use of the large muscles in the body and include activities such as walking, running and climbing
b **Fine manipulative skills** involve the precise use of the hands and fingers such as pointing, drawing, writing, fastening buttons or shoelaces.

Physical development includes **sensory development** – the development of the five senses: sight, touch, hearing, smell and taste. All these senses are important to a child as they develop. We are going to look at sight and hearing.

> Link: *For more information on gross motor and fine manipulative skills see pages 40–43.*

Sight

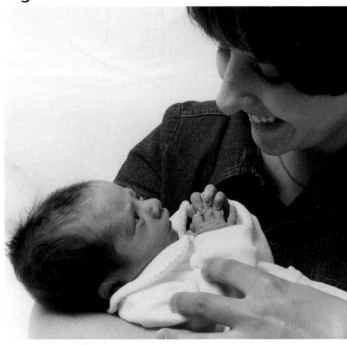

Babies can focus on their mother's or carer's face

At birth, babies can see but cannot focus on objects further than 25 cm away. They are aware of light, darkness and movement and can focus on the mother's or carer's face, for example during feeding

Eyes following a moving toy

At around three months the baby is still short-sighted but can see further. At this age, the baby's eyes will follow people or objects nearby and will spend a lot of time looking at their own hands.

At six months, the eyes begin to work together and babies will start to reach out for objects. By one year, babies can recognize people at a distance, and at eighteen months they realize they are looking at themselves in a mirror. By the age of two and a half years, children can recognize themselves in photographs and by the age of three years they have developed all the visual skills of an adult. At four years a child can match and name four primary colours and by five years can match ten to twelve colours.

Until they start school, a child's eyesight is checked at regular intervals in order to establish that normal progress is being made. Any problems with eyesight can be identified early on and treatment and/or specialist help can then be provided.

Link: For more information on physical disabilities see page 110.

Turning in response to hearing her name

Hearing

Even before birth, research tells us that babies respond to loud noises in the mother's uterus. A newborn baby can recognize the parent's or carer's voice and is startled by loud noises. By three months the baby can respond to their name being called and by six months turns towards a sound, for example their parent's or carer's voice at a distance. At twelve months the baby will recognize familiar sounds and voices, and will know and respond immediately to his or her own name.

By two years of age he or she will listen to general conversation with interest. By the age of four years a child can listen to long stories and by five years a child can hear accurately.

Hearing tests are part of normal developmental screening tests. The development of hearing is an essential part of speech (language) development, and any problems with hearing should be identified as early as possible in order to provide treatment or specialist help so that the child may develop as normally as possible.

Link: For more information on language development and learning difficulties see pages 78–81.

Key points

✦ Physical development involves two main areas called gross motor skills and fine manipulative skills.
✦ The development of the five senses is called sensory development.
✦ Hearing and vision development are checked regularly to identify any problems as early as possible.

Key tasks

1 What is meant by the term 'milestone'?
2 Describe what a baby can see at birth.
3 Why is it important that a baby's hearing is regularly checked?
4 Name two factors on which a child's developmental progress depends.

Further work Design and make a mobile to hang over a baby's cot to encourage sensory development. (RT)

Stages of development (2)

Development of movement

Movement of the body requires the co-ordination of the brain cells with the muscles in the body. Messages from the brain make the muscles work and then the baby will acquire the necessary skills. There is a certain order in which these skills are acquired. Head control is the first to be learnt, followed by the upper body, arms and hand movements and finally the legs.

Gross motor skills

Head control

Newborn babies have neck muscles that are weak and cannot support their heads. When someone is holding the baby, it is important that the head is well supported.

When pulled into a sitting position, a newborn baby's head falls backwards.

By three months the baby can sit with a straighter back if held or supported.

At six months the baby can sit upright with a straight back, but will still need support from someone holding their hands in front or using a cushion or chair behind.

From nine months the baby can sit unsupported for a while and turn the body when reaching out for a toy.

Lying on the stomach (prone position)

A newborn baby will lie with the knees brought up under the abdomen, if placed on its front.

At three months the baby can lift both the head and chest off the floor using the forearms for support.

By six months, when lying on the stomach, the baby can lift the head and chest using its hands and straightened arms as support. At around this age the baby will also start rolling over.

At three months the baby has developed some head control, and when pulled into a sitting position, there is little head lag (falling backwards).

By six months, the baby has full head control, can use the shoulders to pull themselves into a sitting position and can turn the head towards a sound.

Sitting up

In a newborn baby, the muscles in the back are not developed and so the baby cannot sit up.

The baby at nine months can find ways of moving about the floor, e.g. crawling on the stomach.

At one year the baby can crawl on its hands and knees, shuffling along on its bottom or bear-walking (using hands and feet to move).

Most babies crawl before they can walk, but some miss out this stage altogether. This shows the wide variation of normal progression through physical development.

Standing and walking

In order to walk, the muscles in the legs and back need to strengthen and the baby has to learn to keep balance and to co-ordinate all the muscles that are used for walking.

A newborn baby has an automatic reflex action called the walking reflex.

> **Link:** *For more information on newborn reflex actions see pages 34–35.*

By six months a baby can support almost all their weight and, if held in a standing position, can do so with a straight back.

At nine months a baby can pull her/himself into a standing position and can stand and take a few steps whilst holding on to furniture or someone's hands.

At one year, the baby can walk with one hand held. By thirteen months, some babies can walk alone but they may not have good balance.

At fifteen months, most babies can walk alone and can crawl upstairs, although some may have difficulty in coming downstairs backwards.

By eighteen months, the child can walk steadily and stop without sitting down or falling over suddenly. A child of this age will also be able to climb up and down stairs if supported by a rail and by putting both feet on each step. At this age the child will also be able to crawl backwards down the stairs in a safe manner.

At two years the child can run safely, climb onto furniture, throw a ball, walk up and down stairs using both feet on each step, sit on a tricycle and move it with their feet (not pedals). They can also push large toys with wheels and kick a ball

By two and a half years the child can tiptoe and jump with both feet together.

At three years the child can ride a tricycle using pedals, can catch a large ball with arms out-stretched and can go upstairs one foot at a time (but still come down the stairs putting two feet on each step).

By four years of age the child can walk up and down stairs like an adult, ride a tricycle with skill, and can catch, kick and bounce a ball.

By the age of five the child can skip, stand on one foot, hop, and demonstrate good co-ordination when playing games.

Key points

✦ Gross motor skills include activities such as head control, sitting up, crawling and walking.
✦ Children develop at different rates, and it must be remembered that they all go through these stages of physical development in their own time.

Key tasks

1 Why is it important that a newborn baby's head is always supported?
2 What is the average age that a baby acquires the following skills?
   a Full head control.
   b Walking alone.
   c Climbing stairs using a handrail for support.
   d Riding a tricycle using the pedals.

Further work Observe a child's gross motor skills over a three-week period, e.g. crawling, walking, climbing and running. (IT)

Stages of development (3)

Fine manipulative skills

A newborn baby has an automatic reflex action called the grasp reflex.

Link: For more information on the newborn baby see pages 34–37.

By three months, the baby will start to control the hands, will spend time playing with its hands and may hold a rattle for a short time.

At six months, a baby can grasp an object, using the whole hand to pass a toy from one hand to the other.

At nine months, the fingers and thumb are used to grasp an object. This is known as the pincer grasp. At around four weeks later, the baby can pick up small objects with the finger and thumb

At one year, the baby can point with the index finger and place one brick on top of another. By fifteen months, the baby can show a preference for one hand over the other and can grasp a crayon using a whole hand grasp.

At eighteen months, the child can build a tower of three to five bricks, scribble a picture, use a spoon for feeding (messily) and hold a pencil in the whole hand or with the thumb and first two fingers.

The child of two years can build a tower of six or more bricks, draw circles, lines and dots, drink from a cup, turn single pages in a book and, by two and a half years, can build a tower of seven or more bricks and paint a picture.

At three years of age the child can build a tower of about nine or ten bricks, can control a pencil well with the thumb and first two fingers, thread large beads onto a lace, use a fork and spoon to eat with, use scissors to cut paper, and draw a person with a head and sometimes legs.

By four years the child can thread small beads onto a lace, hold and use a pencil as an adult, and draw a figure with head, legs and body.

At the age of five years the child can use a knife and fork for eating, sew large stitches, do jigsaw puzzles, has acquired good pencil control and can draw a person with head, body, legs, arms, nose, mouth and eyes.

Hand–eye co-ordination

The development of hand–eye co-ordination is the ability to connect the movement of the hands with what the eyes can see – the brain controls the muscle movement. Hand–eye co-ordination develops alongside the development of gross motor skills and fine manipulative skills, e.g. a child playing on a climbing frame needs to use his or her eyes to identify where to place hands and feet to tell the brain where to move the limbs. Other activities would include building a tower of bricks, threading beads, drawing and fastening buttons.

The development of teeth

In a newborn baby teeth are already developing in the gums. The average age when teeth begin to emerge is at six months. These teeth are called milk teeth. There will be twenty teeth when they have all come through by the age of three years. Milk teeth usually come through in a certain order (see diagram below).

After the age of five years the milk teeth begin to fall out as the roots disappear. At the age of six years permanent teeth begin to emerge.

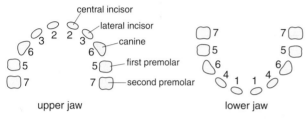

The order in which milk teeth usually appear

Teething

Teething is when the teeth emerge through the gums, and a baby may display a number of signs that teething is taking place:

- chewing on hard objects
- excessive dribbling
- fretfulness
- sore gums or a red cheek.

These problems can be soothed by the parent or carer by:

- providing hard foods to chew on, e.g. carrot or rusks
- cuddling and comforting the baby
- diverting the baby's attention, e.g. playing with a toy or going out.

However, if the baby is very fretful the parent or carer should seek medical advice.

Caring for the teeth

As a rule, sweet, sticky foods should be avoided as they encourage tooth decay. The diet should include foods that are high in calcium to encourage healthy teeth, e.g. milk and cheese, and foods that require chewing, e.g. apples and crusts of bread.

The teeth should be cleaned as soon as they appear using a small amount of toothpaste and a piece of soft fabric such as muslin.

Once the child is one year old they can be given a toothbrush and taught to clean the teeth in an up and down action. Teeth should be cleaned after meals and at bed time. It is important to establish a good teeth cleaning habit early on so it will be continued throughout life.

The dentist

Children should be encouraged to visit the dentist from around the age of three. In this way the child will become used to going and will feel confident about these visits as they get older.

Key points

- ✦ Fine manipulative skills means the development and control of the hands and the fingers.
- ✦ Hand–eye co-ordination is the ability to connect hand movement with what the eyes can see.
- ✦ Caring for a child's teeth is important in preventing tooth decay.

Key tasks

1 What is the average age that a baby acquires the following skills?
   a Demonstrates the pincer grasp.
   b Builds a tower of three to five bricks.
   c Uses scissors to cut paper.
   d Threads small beads.
2 How many milk teeth does an average three-year-old have?
3 Suggest two signs that a baby may be teething.
4 Why is it important that teeth are cleaned on a regular basis?

Further work	1	Design and make a toy using household objects to encourage a fine manipulative skill. Consider the safety of the toy. (RT)
	2	Prepare a suitable snack for a two-year-old child that will encourage healthy teeth. (RT)
	3	Design and make a poster to encourage children to clean their teeth. (RT)

Development conditions

In order for children to grow and develop physically, certain conditions should be provided by the parents and carers. These conditions include:

+ warmth
+ rest, exercise and fresh air
+ routine
+ regular sleeping patterns
+ cleanliness
+ the housing environment.

Warmth

All children need to be kept warm, especially newborn babies. Older children still require warmth, but they do not require such close attention as a newborn. This is because they can maintain their own body temperature more efficiently than a newborn baby.

Rest, exercise and fresh air

Children enjoying fresh air and exercise

It is important to maintain a balance of rest and exercise for children. They should be encouraged to play outside as much as possible. If the child has access to a garden, this provides a space to play. If there is no garden, regular trips to a park or play area are necessary so that the child can have the opportunity to practice physical skills such as running and climbing. Fresh air and plenty of exercise will encourage the child to sleep soundly and develop a healthy appetite.

Routine

A routine may be difficult to establish with a young baby, so it is often easier for a mother to fit in with the baby's natural pattern of feeding and sleeping to begin with. As the baby gets older, it is important to establish a routine for sleeping, feeding, bathing, and so on, to provide the child with a sense of security and to fit in with family life. By the age of one year the child will have some understanding of a routine.

Regular sleeping patterns

It is important that a child has a regular bedtime routine because an established routine will help a child to feel secure. A story at bedtime on a regular basis will help establish this routine. The child may prefer a night light or the bedroom door to be left open. Many children need a comforter or favourite toy to provide a sense of security.

Babies need a lot of sleep, but as the child gets older less sleep is needed. Most children have a rest or nap during the day, until this is dropped at around the age of three years old and the child will be sleeping for about twelve hours a night.

Cleanliness

Babies and children need to be kept clean. Babies do not need to have a daily bath – some days 'topping and tailing' will be sufficient (this is when a baby's face, hands and bottom are washed).

Bathing a baby

It is important that everything needed for bathing is collected together first so that all items are within easy reach. A baby or young child must never be left in the bath unsupervised. The water temperature should be around 37°C and should

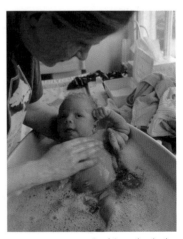

Bathing the baby

be tested with the adult's elbow to ensure it is not too hot. Use the following guidelines for bathing a young baby:

+ undress the baby (leave the nappy on for the moment) and wrap in a towel to keep her or him warm
+ wipe the baby's face with damp cotton wool. Do not use soap
+ wipe the eyes with a clean piece of cotton wool for each eye to prevent the spread of any infection
+ wash the baby's scalp, using a mild shampoo
+ unwrap the baby from the towel and remove the nappy, cleaning away any mess
+ gently lower the baby into the water, supporting the neck, and wash gently
+ lift the baby out of the water and pat dry, being careful to dry the creases in the neck, groin, armpits and the backs of the legs.

Bathtime should be an enjoyable experience, and can be built into the child's bedtime routine if that suits the family.

Changing nappies

Ensure that this is always carried out on a flat surface and that an older baby cannot roll off. Nappy cream or zinc and castor oil will offer some protection against the moisture in a nappy and help prevent nappy rash.

Nappy rash

Nappy rash is caused by ammonia that is produced when urine comes into contact with bacteria (germs). This causes the skin to go red with a rash which, if left untreated, can become very sore and cause great discomfort to the baby. To avoid nappy rash follow these guidelines:

+ change the nappy frequently
+ leave the nappy off if possible for some time during the day
+ never leave a dirty nappy on for any length of time
+ thoroughly clean the baby's skin at each nappy change
+ use a nappy cream to protect the skin.

Learning bladder and bowel control

As with all areas of development, children learn to control their bladder and bowel at different times. The earliest age is usually around sixteen months old. Bowel control is likely to be learnt before bladder control and can only begin when a child starts to control the muscles which open the bladder and the bowel. Parents and carers can help the child by:

+ not rushing the process – the child needs to be ready to co-operate and be aware of having a wet or dirty nappy
+ not pressurizing the child into using the potty or toilet before they are ready
+ providing praise and encouragement for progress
+ encouraging good hygiene habits, e.g. washing hands after using the toilet.

The housing environment

The type of housing that a child is brought up in will have an effect on their overall development. The child who lives in cramped, damp conditions in buildings that are condemned as dangerous can suffer ill health. This may lead to their progress in development being hindered or slowed down. The child's safety is also put at risk. The child needs to be brought up in a warm, safe and secure environment in order to reach his or her full potential in all areas of development.

Key points

+ There are many conditions that a parent or carer should provide for their children in order for them to grow and develop.
+ It is important that children have sleep, exercise and cleanliness included in their daily routine.

Key tasks

1 What conditions should a parent or carer provide in order for the child to grow and develop?
2 Why is it important that the child has plenty of rest, exercise and fresh air?
3 Describe briefly how to bath a baby.
4 Explain the importance of toilet training being carefully handled by the parent or carer.

Clothing and footwear for babies and children

There is a wide variety of clothing available for children and there are certain factors to consider when buying these items for babies and children. These include whether the clothing is:

+ hard wearing
+ easy for the child to put on and take off
+ loose enough for movement.

Link: *For more information on clothing see page 121.*

A selection of clothing will be necessary for night time, playtime and to suit the climate, e.g. for hot, wet and cold weather.

Nightwear

A selection of nightwear

By law, children's nightwear must have a flameproof finish to the fabric so that the garment will not catch fire easily. Nightwear must be loose, comfortable and warm, with no ribbons that may get caught around the child's neck or wrists. Pyjamas are ideal for children for comfort and accessibility for the toilet. Nighties can be cool for hot weather if made from cotton.

Outdoor clothing

Outdoor garments need to be made from hard-wearing fabrics such as denim or corduroy. Weatherproof clothing is useful against the cold and wet weather, as are padded coats and all-in-one suits. Clothing for outdoors should be loose enough to allow movement.

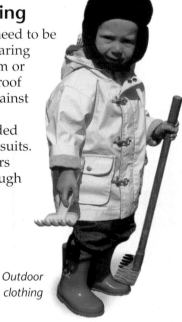

Outdoor clothing

Play clothes

Play or day clothes should be hard wearing and easily washable – active children will easily make their clothes dirty, and these will require frequent washing.

Hard-wearing play clothes

Footwear

Babies do not require footwear until they are walking. Feet need to be protected against damage and to keep them warm. However, going barefoot is very healthy for feet as it encourages the feet to grow strong. 'Padders' keep babies' feet cosy and offer protection when crawling.

'Padders' are suitable for babies who can't yet walk

Older children require correctly fitting shoes in order for their feet to grow and develop naturally. Children's feet can be damaged by poorly fitting shoes as the bones in the feet are soft and grow very quickly – never allow a child to wear tight shoes or other children's shoes.

Feet should be measured regularly every three months. Shoes should be bought from shops that offer a free fitting service and have trained fitters who offer help and advice. A wide variety of styles are available in a range of sizes, half sizes and different widths.

The process of buying shoes can be a lengthy one, and shoe shops sometimes have an activity corner or an area where children can play with a selection of toys.

Parents and carers should consider the following points when choosing footwear for children:

+ leather fabric is hard wearing and allows the foot to breathe
+ is there room for growth?
+ the shoe should offer protection and support to the foot

+ it should have an adjustable fastening
+ the sole should be flexible and anti-slip.

A selection of footwear

Parents and carers should be aware that a child's socks and tights also need to be checked regularly to ensure that they are not too tight – this can also damage the feet in the same way as tight shoes. Socks and tights should be changed as the feet grow and develop.

Key points

+ Parents and carers need to be aware of the wide variety of clothing available, but to be selective when buying clothing, so that whatever is bought suits the weather and situation.
+ Footwear is extremely important and should be well fitted and checked regularly to ensure that feet can grow and develop in the correct way.

Key tasks

1 What points should be considered when purchasing children's clothing?
2 What does the law say about children's nightwear?
3 Explain why it is important that children should wear correctly fitting shoes.

Further work	Investigate the variety of children's clothing available in different outlets. Record your findings and find out the cost. (RT)

Nutrition (1)

Nutrition is a study of the nutrients found in the foods in our diet. An understanding of nutrition is important, as parents and carers need to use this knowledge when providing healthy and nutritious food for babies and young children.

Nutrients

The function of nutrients includes:

+ to help the body grow and repair
+ to provide energy in order to carry out physical activity
+ to keep the body warm
+ to help carry out other essential processes such as digestion.

Foods usually contain more than one nutrient. For example, milk contains protein, fat, carbohydrate, vitamins and minerals.

The macronutrients

The word **macronutrient** is used to explain nutrients that the body needs in large amounts. Proteins, carbohydrates and fats are macronutrients.

Protein

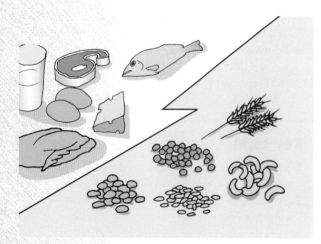

Protein comes from animal and plant sources

Protein is needed for the growth and repair of body tissues such as the blood cells and muscles. Babies and young children grow rapidly and the protein needs of a child are high. Protein-rich foods come from both animal and vegetable sources. Some high protein foods are expensive, and cheaper sources can be just as nutritious.

Protein complementation

Proteins are made up of smaller units called **amino acids**. There are many different types of amino acids. For a protein to be of use to the body to grow new tissues, the right amount and proportion of amino acids needs to be eaten.

Animal protein sources contain all the amino acids needed to build tissue. These amino acids are called the indispensable amino acids. These animal sources of protein are referred as of high biological value (HBV).

Vegetable protein sources, such as cereals and pulses, contain some but not all of the indispensable amino acids. Vegetable sources of protein are called of low biological value (LBV).

If two different vegetable sources of protein are eaten together in a meal such as a pulse (beans) with a cereal (toast), all the indispensable amino acids will be present and the meal will be of high biological value.

Combining sources of protein in this way is called protein complementation.

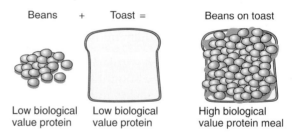

The complementation of proteins

An understanding of the complementation of proteins is particularly important for babies and young children on a vegetarian diet.

Carbohydrates

Carbohydrate foods provide the body with energy. Types of carbohydrates are:

+ sugars, which are found in fruits, cakes, biscuits and soft drinks
+ starches, such as potatoes, bread, pasta and rice.

Sugars

Sugar is added to many foods during their manufacture or during the preparation of food in the home. In fruit and some vegetables sugar is found in the form of glucose and fructose, while in cereals it is found as maltose and in milk as lactose.

Starches

Starches are good sources of energy in the diet because, unlike sugar, they are found with other nutrients. For example, they are found in bread, which also contains proteins, vitamins, minerals and dietary fibre (NSP). Therefore, it is a healthier option for young children to get their energy from starch. Starches have always been a large part of children's diet in the United Kingdom and they are often referred to as staple foods.

When starch sources such as wheat and rice are processed, they lose some of their nutrients and dietary fibre. Less processed starch products, such as wholewheat flour, are therefore more nutritious.

Dietary fibre

Dietary fibre is a form of carbohydrate, which is not used for energy. It is also called non-starch polysaccharide (NSP) or cellulose. It is found in raw plant material, in the outer coating of cereals and in the structure of fruit and vegetables – it is the tough fibrous part of plants. The body cannot digest dietary fibre so it passes through the body absorbing water and increasing in bulk. This helps stimulate the digestive system to work properly and to avoid constipation.

Fats

Fats are the most concentrated form of energy. They are found in food products such as butter, oil and cream. Fats are also present in other foods such as cheese, cakes and chocolate, and in fried foods such as chips, where they are referred to as invisible fats.

Although fats are a useful source of energy, too much fat can be harmful because of other substances associated with fats. This is true of cholesterol, which is linked to health problems such as coronary heart disease and high blood pressure. It is found mainly with fat products from animal sources such as butter and eggs.

Fat has the following functions in the body:

+ it provides a concentrated source of energy
+ it provides us with Vitamins A and D
+ it is stored in the tissues and keeps us warm.

Young children need a certain amount of fat to function, but if the intake is too high they will store the surplus as body fat and put on weight.

Key points

+ Foods contain a range of nutrients.
+ Macronutrients are foods that the body needs in large amounts.
+ Protein is needed for the growth and repair of body tissues.
+ Fats and carbohydrates provide the body with energy.
+ Dietary fibre (NSP) helps the digestive system work properly.

Key tasks

1 Explain the term 'protein complementation'.
2 Why are unprocessed sources of carbohydrate, such as wholewheat flour, better for young children?
3 Explain why young children need a high intake of protein.

Further work | Use a nutrition database to compare the nutritional value of white bread and wholewheat bread. Use ICT to display your results. (RT/IT)

Nutrition (2)

Micronutrients

Micronutrients are the vitamins and minerals that are needed in much smaller quantities. Just because they are only needed in small amounts does not mean that they are not important to the body. Vitamins and minerals carry out a number of essential functions in the body. They often work with other nutrients to carry these out functions (see table below).

The functions of vitamins and minerals

Nutrient	Sources	Functions
Vitamin A	Whole milk, butter, margarine, eggs, cheese, oily fish, carrots, green vegetables	Keeps skin and mucous tissues healthy. Helps eyesight
Vitamin B complex (all the group of B vitamins such as thiamin and folic acid)	Bread and wholegrain cereals, liver, milk and milk products	Helps the release of energy from food
Vitamin C	Citrus and other fruits, vegetables	Helps maintain the connective tissues that form the structure of tissue, such as muscle, in the body. Helps the healing of wounds. Helps the absorption of iron
Vitamin D	Milk, margarine, butter, liver; also comes from exposure to the sun	Works with calcium to form healthy bones and teeth
Calcium	Milk, butter, yoghurt, white bread, dried fruit, sardines	Essential for the formation of strong bones and teeth. Helps with blood clotting. Assists muscle contraction
Sodium	Bacon, sausages, crisps, cheese; also added to foods as salt during cooking	Needed in all body fluids to maintain fluid balance
Iron	Meat, liver, kidney, bread, green vegetables, dried fruit and pulses	Forms part of the haemoglobin in the blood, which carries oxygen around the body
Fluoride	Drinking water, seafood, fluoride toothpaste	Helps in the formation of bones and teeth and helps them resist decay

Deficiency diseases

Deficiency diseases are caused by a shortage of a nutrient. Anaemia is a deficiency disease caused by a lack of iron in the diet. A low intake of calcium will mean that less calcium is deposited in the bones, which will lead to weakness in the skeleton. Severe calcium shortage could result in rickets.

Dietary reference values

The amount of nutrients needed by babies and young children in their diet is calculated using **dietary reference values (DRVs)**. DRVs are measures of the amounts of a nutrient or energy needed by a person to be healthy.

DRVs are calculated as daily average amounts for population groups. Population groups means a group of people with similar nutritional and energy needs such as two-year-old children. It is important to know how nutritional values are calculated using DRVs to help understand the value of foods in the diet.

There are a range of different DRV measures such as reference nutrient intake (RNI) and estimated average requirement (EAR):

✦ reference nutrient intake (RNI). This is the amount of a nutrient, e.g. protein, that is needed by a population group. For example, the RNI for a four- to six-month-old baby is 12.7 grams of protein per day (see table below). This means that a baby of this age needs that amount of protein for the growth and repair of their body

Reference nutrient intake (RNI) of protein for children under six years of age

Age of child	Grams/day
4–6 months	12.7
7–9 months	13.7
10–12 months	14.9
1–3 years	15.5
4–6 years	19.7

✦ estimated average requirement (EAR). This is an estimate of the average requirements for a population group such as a twelve-month-old baby. As it is the average it means that some babies will need more than the EAR and some will need less. The following table shows the amount of kilocalories/kilojoules needed to provide for the energy needs of babies and young children.

EAR of kilocalories/kilojoules for children under six years of age

Age of child	Girls		Boys	
	KJ/day	Kcal/day	KJ/day	Kcal/day
0–3 months	2280	545	2160	515
4–6 months	2890	690	2690	645
7–9 months	3340	825	3200	765
10–12 months	3850	920	3610	865
1–3 years	5150	1230	4860	1165
4–6 years	7160	1715	6460	1545

The energy value of foods

All macronutrients, protein, fats and carbohydrates provide the body with some energy. Fats provide twice as much energy as carbohydrates and proteins, so fat is the most concentrated source of energy. All these nutrients are broken down and used by the body to provide energy for:

+ activities
+ keeping our body temperature maintained
+ other body processes such as growth and repair, breathing and other body systems such as circulation.

Children vary in the amount of energy they need because:

+ some children are more active than others
+ boys have a higher basal metabolic rate than girls. This means that they use up energy at a faster rate than girls
+ age and size or height will affect the amount of energy needed by the body.

Measuring energy in food

The energy in food is measured in kilocalories (kcal) or kilojoules (kJ).

1 kilocalorie = 4.2 kilojoules

Kilocalories can be converted to kilojoules by multiplying by 4.2. Food labels on baby and toddler food products usually give the energy value of the product in both kilocalories and kilojoules.

Energy balance

If young children eat more kilocalories than they use up in energy, they will put on additional weight. There are many overweight young children today because they have a diet that is high in energy-dense foods such as chips and sweets, and high fat, fast foods such as burgers. To maintain an energy balance during childhood, it is necessary to balance the kilocalories taken in as food with the kilocalories used as energy for activities. When there is an energy imbalance, the body will become overweight or underweight.

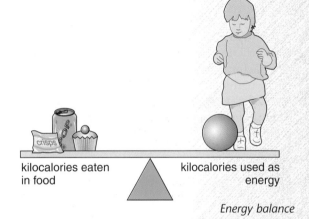

kilocalories eaten in food   kilocalories used as energy

Energy balance

Key points

+ Vitamins and minerals are micronutrients and are needed in small amounts by the body.
+ Deficiency diseases are caused by a shortage of a nutrient.
+ Dietary reference values (DRVs) are measures of the amount of a nutrient or energy needed.
+ To maintain an energy balance the kilocalories taken in as food needs to be balanced with the kilocalories used as energy for activities.

Key tasks

1 What are dietary reference values?
2 Why is it important to maintain an energy balance?
3 Explain why the energy requirements of babies and young children will vary.

Healthy eating

Dietary goals

Dietary goals are targets that are set to improve the health of people in the United Kingdom.

Diet-related illnesses

Many diseases today are related to our eating habits. They are called **diet-related illnesses** for this reason. Healthy eating habits that are established while children are young will reduce their chances of developing a diet-related illness such as coronary heart disease. Diets that are high in calories and fat and low in dietary fibre may result in health problems such as obesity, coronary heart disease and diabetes in later life. One factor thought to trigger diabetes mellitus is overweight. Diabetes is when the body has a high level of glucose in the blood. Diabetes mellitus is a form of diabetes that develops later in life and is related to diet. This can lead to damage to the kidneys, nervous system and the heart.

Heart disease

Heart disease covers a range of conditions varying from coronary heart disease and strokes to hypertension:

+ coronary heart disease and strokes. These are linked to many factors, one of which is a high level of cholesterol in the blood. The liver uses the fat we eat to produce cholesterol. This is a fat-like substance that gets deposited on the walls of the arteries when the level of blood cholesterol is high. The arteries become narrower and restrict the flow of blood around the body. In some cases this can lead to a heart attack. Other factors thought to contribute to coronary heart disease and strokes are:
  + being overweight
  + high blood pressure
  + smoking
  + lack of activity.

Healthy artery allows blood to flow   Artery narrowed by cholesterol deposits

+ hypertension. This is often referred to as high blood pressure and means that a person's blood pressure is very high. The blood is forced through the arteries at a higher pressure than normal and this puts extra strain on the heart. Hypertension can be caused by high cholesterol and high levels of salt in the diet. It can lead to heart attacks. People with hypertension need to follow a low fat and low salt diet.

Low fibre diets

It is estimated that over a third of the population of the UK has too low an intake of dietary fibre (NSP). Dietary fibre is needed to make sure the digestive system functions properly and to prevent bowel conditions such as constipation, diverticular disease and bowel cancer. Diets that rely on prepared food products are more likely to be low in fibre.

Childhood obesity

Children's diet affects their health both in the long and short term. The number of children who are overweight is increasing – it is estimated that one child in five is overweight. The term 'obesity' refers to a person whose weight is at least a third more than the average weight for their age and size.

Many foods that appeal to young children are very energy-dense and nutrient scarce, such as high sugar drinks. This means that they are high in calories but low in other nutrients. Young children do need high levels of energy, but it is better to obtain this energy from foods that also contain other nutrients, such as brown bread, pasta and other cereals. If a child eats food containing more calories than they use in energy, they will put on weight.

Children who are overweight become less active and this can lead to further weight gain. The extra weight can put a strain on the heart and blood circulation, which can in turn, lead to other health problems later in life. Many children are overweight because they have too high an intake of sugar and fat.

Energy dense and nutrient scarce foods

Sugar in the diet

Children like sweet tastes. Breast and formula milk does have a sweet taste because of the lactose present in it. Sugar is often called an empty calorie food because it provides the body with energy but not with any other nutrients. Most sweet products that children like have sugar added in the manufacturing process. These sugars are called extrinsic sugars (added sugars) and can be harmful to their teeth. Natural sugars present in foods such as fruit and vegetables are less harmful to the teeth.

Food product	Teaspoons of sugar per portion
Cocoa	3
Flavoured yoghurt	2
Cheese sandwich on white bread	4
Jelly and ice cream	4
Can of Coke	6
Baked beans	2
Chocolate crispy cereal	2
Burger in a bun	2
Ketchup	1
Tinned fruit in syrup	5
Fresh orange juice	3

Levels of sugar in foods

How is sugar harmful to the teeth?

Diets that are high in sugar can cause **plaque** to form. Plaque is formed when bacteria in the mouth convert the sugar to acid. This can attack the enamel of the teeth, causing dental cavities.

> **Link:** *For more information on caring for the teeth see page 43.*

Parents and carers should follow these guidelines to help reduce sugar levels in the diet of children:

+ give young children diluted, unsweetened fruit juices to reduce the sugar levels, rather than squashes and fizzy drinks
+ avoid adding extra sugar to hot drinks such as cocoa
+ limit the amount of sweet foods such as chocolate, biscuits and cakes the baby or young child eats
+ substitute sugary foods with other snacks that are low in sugar, such as pieces of fresh fruit or vegetables, unsweetened yoghurts or savoury biscuits.

Key tasks

1 Explain the term 'diet-related illness'.
2 Describe the causes of:
   a Coronary heart disease.
   b Hypertension.
   c Diverticular disease.
3 Why is too much sugar unhealthy for young children?

Further work

Record the food you eat over two days and identify which of these foods contain sugar. Write a brief report to comment on the amount of sugar you ate. (RT/IT)

A balanced diet

Healthy eating habits in childhood should help reduce the risk of diet-related illnesses in later life. It is important that parents and carers understand the concepts of nutrition so they can plan a **balanced diet** for their children. A balanced diet is a diet that contains the right amount and proportions of nutrients. Dietary reference values can be used to help make sure the diet of a child is nutritionally sound.

> **Link:** *For more information on dietary reference values see pages 50–51.*

Healthy eating guidelines

There are many approaches to planning healthy diets for children. The *Balance of Good Health* is a guide to food selection that has been developed by the Health Education Authority. It provides a visual picture of the foods to choose for a healthy diet and shows the proportion of one food group to another for healthy eating. For example, it shows that we should be eating a high proportion of fruits and vegetables and cereals, and lower proportions of dairy products.

The National Food Guide
The Balance of Good Health

Fruit and vegetables
Choose a wide variety

Bread, other cereals and potatoes
Eat all types and choose high fibre kinds whenever you can

Meat, fish and alternatives
Choose lower fat alternatives whenever you can

Fatty and sugary foods
Try not to eat these too often, and when you do, have small amounts

Milk and dairy foods
Choose lower fat alternatives whenever you can

The Balance of Good Health

The *Balance of Good Health* supports the government's guidelines for a healthy diet. These are:

+ enjoy your food
+ eat a variety of different foods
+ eat plenty of foods that are rich in starch and fibre

+ don't eat too many foods that contain a lot of fat
+ don't have sugary foods and drinks too often
+ look after the vitamins and minerals in your food.

These healthy eating guidelines are not intended to apply in full to young children under five. This is because they have high energy requirements for their body weight. However, a sensible family eating pattern based on these guidelines will encourage children to eat more healthily at home, because eating habits are established when children are young.

Planning meals

The key points to consider when planning meals for children:

+ include proteins, calcium, iron, and vitamins A and D which are essential for growing children. The rapid growth of early childhood requires nutrient-dense foods that are rich in essential macro-and micronutrients
+ include high fibre food in their diet in a form that is appropriate for their age. Vegetables and fruits will be puréed during the early stages of weaning, but firmer textures should be gradually introduced for a toddler to learn to chew properly
+ whole milk is recommended for children as a main drink. Semi-skimmed and skimmed milk do not provide enough energy or vitamin A. Semi-skimmed milk may be given to children over the age of two
+ a variety of foods should be given to children at an early age to get them used to a range of tastes and textures, as **food preferences** (the foods a child likes or dislikes) are established in early childhood
+ choose healthier methods of cooking such as grilling or baking rather than frying as frying adds extra fat
+ young children need plenty of liquids to maintain their fluid balance. They should be encouraged to drink water and unsweetened drinks as well as milk, rather than fizzy and sugary drinks
+ mealtimes should be regular with limited snack foods in between

◆ young children have small appetites. Serve small, attractive portions – they can always have more later

◆ make family meals happy, social occasions that the young child will look forward to and enjoy

◆ encourage children to be independent in feeding themselves as early as possible.

Learning to feed themselves

When young children start learning to feed themselves they will get very messy. Parents and carers can help young children to learn by providing small cutlery and a dish with straight sides for the child to push the food up against. With encouragement a young child will soon learn to feed itself.

When children learn to feed themselves they get messy

At twelve months babies will mainly use their hands to feed themselves. By two years they can use a spoon well and may manage a fork. They can lift up a cup with two hands. By the time they are three years old they can use a fork and spoon with precision. When they are four years old they can use a knife, fork and spoon and serve themselves from dishes. They may still need help cutting up difficult food.

Prepared food products

Modern family lifestyles have cut down on the time available for cooking meals. Many parents and carers have limited time to cook and prepare meals and rely on prepared food products. Many prepared food products are high in fat and sugar. However, some can be used as part of a balanced diet. Prepared food products that can be easily and quickly cooked include baked beans, fish fingers, tinned fish and wholegrain breakfast cereals. Advice about the use of prepared food products includes:

◆ read the labels carefully to understand what they contain

◆ use with fresh foods

◆ avoid any products that are high in fat, salt or sugar

◆ try to add additional textures to serve with the products

◆ grill, bake or microwave the products instead of frying.

For further reference

Nursery milk scheme – children attending nursery school are entitled to receive a third of a pint of free milk for every day they attend.

Welfare food scheme – children under the age of five whose parents receive Income Support are eligible to receive a free pint of milk daily.

More information about milk initiative in schools can be found on the National Dairy Council website at www.milk.co.uk

Key tasks

1 Explain why young children should drink whole milk.

2 What is the *Balance of Good Health*? Explain how it can be used to plan healthy, balanced meals for young children.

3 Prepare a checklist to identify the key points to consider when planning meals for young children.

Further work	1 Plan meals for a three-year-old child for a day using the *Balance of Good Health*. Explain and justify the decisions you have made about food choice. (RT)
	2 Create a design for a simple jigsaw or domino game for a four-year-old child to help them understand about healthy eating. (RT/IT)

Feeding the newborn baby

Breastfeeding

Food is a basic need of a newborn baby. Babies are born with a natural reflex to suck. If a baby is put to its mother's breast after birth, it will start to suck. The first milk from the mother's breast is **colostrom**. This is a protein-rich liquid that also contains antibodies from the mother to protect the baby from infection. The colostrum is produced for two or three days after the birth, when the breast first starts to produce milk.

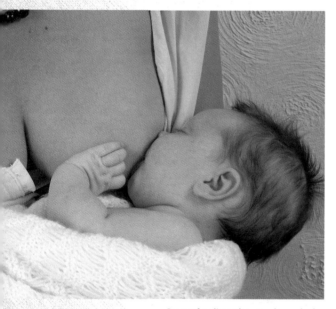

Breastfeeding the newborn baby

Nutritional requirements of a newborn baby

Breast milk can supply all the nutrients a baby needs. Breast milk differs in composition from cow's milk, which is not suitable for babies. This is because it contains different proportions of the nutrients. **Formula milk** is the name given to manufactured milks and milk powders designed for babies, and is the only alternative to breast milk for babies up to the age of six months. Formula milks are modified to make sure they contain the correct nutritional balance for a baby (see table opposite).

Choice of milk

The nutritional value of different milks per 100g

Nutrient	Breast	Formula	Cow's
Protein (g)	1.2	1.5	3.3
Fat (g)	3.8	3.6	3.7
Carbohydrate (g)	7	7.2	4.8
Sodium (mg)	15	15	58
Calcium (mg)	125	44	44
Phosphorus (mg)	15	30	96
Iron (mg)	0.08	0.12	0.10
Vitamin A (µg)	58	79	40
Vitamin C (µg)	4.3	5.6	1.6
Vitamin D (µg)	0.01	1.1	1.6

Cow's milk is not suitable for young babies as it has more protein and salt (sodium) than breast milk. High levels of sodium can be harmful to a baby. One of the proteins in milk is called casein and cow's milk has a higher proportion of casein, which babies find difficult to digest. Formula milk is usually made from cow's milk, but it has been modified to contain less casein and make it suitable for babies. Formula milk is similar in nutritional value to breast milk.

Formula milk products

The choice of feeding method

The mother will have made the decision whether to breast or bottle feed during pregnancy. There are many factors that may affect the decision she makes. Sometimes the decision will be made for practical reasons such as the mother's return to work. Many mothers will use both methods of feeding, starting with breastfeeding and moving on to bottle feeding or using bottle feeding to supplement the breastfeeds. Some factors that may affect the decision about the choice of feeding method include:

+ cost
+ mother's employment pattern
+ parents' or carer's lifestyles
+ personal viewpoint of parents
+ cultural background.

The nursing mother

Breastfeeding is considered to be the best method for feeding because breast milk is ideally suited to the baby. A breast-feeding mother is often called a nursing mother or she is said to be **lactating** because she is feeding milk to the baby. The production of milk in the breasts is triggered by the birth of the baby. Nursing mothers should make sure their diet contains calcium-rich foods and plenty of fluid. Substances taken by the nursing mother will be absorbed into her body and passed to the feeding baby, so alcohol and medicines should be avoided whenever possible.

Advantages of breastfeeding:

+ it is free and convenient
+ it helps the development of a bond between mother and baby as they spend a lot of time in close physical contact with each other
+ it helps the mother's uterus return to shape after pregnancy as it stimulates the hormone that controls this
+ it uses up 1300 kilocalories a day, which helps the mother to return to her previous weight.

Feeding routines

Breastfed babies are often fed on demand – that is to say, when they are hungry. This means many feeds when the baby is newborn, perhaps up to ten a day. However, after the first few weeks the baby will settle down to a regular pattern of feeding. This will mean about six feeds in 24 hours, depending on the birth weight of the baby. Low birth weight babies need smaller feeds. Gradually the intervals between the feeds get longer, until at about three months the baby no longer needs a night feed. Breast milk is the perfect food for babies because:

+ it provides the correct amount of nutrients for the baby
+ it is easier for the baby to digest
+ it contains antibodies to protect the baby from infections
+ breastfed babies have less chance of having gastroenteritis than bottle fed babies
+ it helps reduce the risks of allergies and diseases such as eczema in young children
+ it is a convenient way of feeding the baby – milk is always at the right temperature, is clean and available.

Key points

+ Babies are born with a natural reflex to suck.
+ Breast milk supplies all the nutrients a baby requires.
+ Formula milks are modified to make sure they contain the right amounts of nutrients for babies.
+ A range of factors will affect the decision whether or not to breastfeed.

Key tasks

1 What is the function of colostrom?
2 Explain why cow's milk is unsuitable for the newborn baby.
3 Explain the factors that will influence the mother's choice of feeding method.

Further work	Carry out a survey to find out about attitudes to breastfeeding. Present your findings in a short report. (RT/IT)

Bottle feeding

Some mothers choose to bottle feed their babies. If the baby is correctly bottle-fed there is no reason why they should not thrive and develop in the same way as a breastfed baby.

There are a wide range of infant formula milks on the market, all modified to provide the correct nutrients for a baby. Products are designed for babies of various ages, with the proportions of the different nutrients modified according to the age of the baby.

> Link: *For more information on formula milk see page 56.*

Parents and carers need to be able to calculate the correct amount of feed for their baby. Calculation charts can be found on all formula milk products (see table below).

Formula milks

Most formula milks are in powder form and need making up into a feed. Instructions on how to do this are given on the formula milk product. It is very important that the instructions are followed. If too much formula milk powder is used to make up the feed the nutrients will be too concentrated. This can cause the baby to put on too much weight. It could also cause more serious side affects such as loss of consciousness, as the baby will be getting too high a level of sodium. Some formula milks are in liquid form and are ready to use.

Making up a formula milk feed

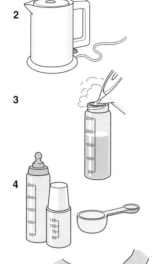

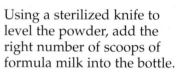

1. Wash hands before starting and ensure all equipment has been washed and sterilized.

2. Boil water for feed and allow it to cool down.

3. Pour cooled boiled water into the feeding bottle up to the appropriate measure level.

4.

5. Using a sterilized knife to level the powder, add the right number of scoops of formula milk into the bottle.

6. Place the cap on the feeding bottle and shake to dissolve the milk powder.

7. Either store the bottle in the fridge until it is needed (but do not keep any made-up milk for longer than 24 hours) or cool it to the correct temperature (approximately 37°C). Test the temperature of the milk on the inside of the wrist before use.

Feeding guide for formula milk products

Approximate age of baby	Approximate weight of baby (kg/lb)	Number of level scoops of powder	Amount of boiled water (fl oz)	Number of feeds in 24 hours
Birth	3.5/7.5	3	3	6
2 weeks	4.0/8.8	4	4	6
2 months	5.0/11.0	5	5	5
4 months	6.5/14.5	7	7	5
6 months	7.5/16.5	8	8	4

Feeding bottles

A wide variety of feeding bottles are available, which have been designed for ease of use. Well designed feeding bottles have:

+ a wide neck for easy cleaning
+ graduated measures on the side, which are easy to read
+ a special cap to keep the teat clean
+ clear plastic that helps to check that it is clean.

Sterilizing feeding equipment

For the baby's first year, all feeding equipment should be sterilized to prevent bacteria spreading an infection to the baby. The sterilizing process is usually carried out using chemical, microwave or electric steam sterilizing equipment. The instructions for sterilizing the equipment must be followed carefully. All the equipment used when preparing feeds, including any brushes that are used to clean the teats and bottles, should be sterilized.

How to bottle feed a baby

The following guidelines advise on how to bottle feed a baby:

+ prepare the feed and warm the bottle if necessary by standing it in some hot water
+ check that the teat hole is not blocked
+ hold the baby in a comfortable position and place the teat in the baby's mouth
+ make sure the bottle is tilted so that it is always full of milk, otherwise the baby will take in air which can give it wind
+ let the baby feed at their own pace
+ the baby may need to bring up wind during the feed – one way of doing this is by holding the baby against a shoulder and rubbing his or her back gently
+ at the end of the feed, throw away any milk that is left.

A feeding pattern for the bottle-fed baby will develop in a similar way to that of the breastfed baby. Some bottle-fed babies are fed on schedule, which means at regular times rather than when the baby feels hungry. A close bond with the parents and carers who feed the baby will build up.

Some young babies have been left with a bottle propped up against a pillow – sometimes called **prop feeding**. This is a dangerous practice as a young baby could choke.

Advantages of bottle feeding:

+ the mother can see exactly how much milk the baby is taking
+ other people besides the mother can feed the baby and build up a bond with the baby
+ babies can be fed anywhere without possible embarrassment
+ it is less tiring for some mothers than breastfeeding.

Key points

+ Choose the correct type of formula milk for the age of the baby.
+ Accurately measure the correct amount of feed.
+ Make sure all feeding equipment is thoroughly washed and sterilized.
+ When feeding the baby, hold the bottle at the correct angle to prevent wind.

Key tasks

1 Explain the advantages of bottle feeding for a mother who is going back to work after her baby is born.
2 Prepare an instruction sheet to describe how to make up a bottle feed for a two-month-old baby.
3 Why is it important to follow the instructions carefully when sterilizing feeding equipment?

Further work

1 Carry out research to find out the range of different formula milk products that are available and their cost. Present your findings to the class. (RT)
2 Find out the cost of a formula milk product. Calculate the cost of feeding a two-week-old baby for a week. (RT)

Weaning

Milk provides all the food a baby needs for at least the first four months of life. As babies gain weight and grow older they need a more varied diet. The changeover from milk to more solid food is called **weaning** or **mixed feeding**.

Signs that a baby is ready to start weaning are when he or she:

+ appears restless or hungry after a feed
+ starts waking at night when they have previously slept through
+ appears to want to be fed more often.

When a baby first starts to be weaned, milk will continue to provide most of the nutrients it needs. As the baby grows older, solid food will gradually become a more important part of its diet and the amount of milk given can be reduced. Weaning is a gradual process, with new foods being introduced slowly one at a time.

Babies are introduced to new foods slowly

Stages of weaning

Stage 1

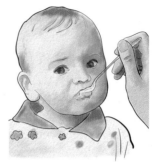

Young babies cannot chew and the first weaning foods will need to be of a similar consistency to milk. Baby cereal such as rice mixed with formula milk is a suitable first weaning food. The food can be given on a spoon and should be at the same temperature as their usual milk feed. Vegetable and fruit purées made to the same smooth consistency are also suitable foods

Stage 2

As babies get used to spoon-feeding they will take more solid food. They can begin to have the same food as the rest of the family, mashed or puréed. Babies are able to chew at six months so can be given some hard foods to chew. These are called finger foods and include items such as rusks and slices of peeled apple. Babies will start to pick up food to put in their mouths at this age

Stage 3

By the age of nine months to one year, the baby will probably be eating solid foods with a top-up milk drink from a feeder cup. A wide variety of foods should be given with a range of textures, because the baby can now cope with food that is lumpier in texture

Food products for weaning

Weaning foods can be easily and simply prepared at home by sieving, liquidizing or mashing foods. Food prepared for weaning the baby should not have extra salt or sugar added. The flavour of the food itself is enough for a baby – flavours that are too strong at this stage may affect the baby's sense of taste for different foods. A wide range of food products suitable for weaning babies at different stages are available in supermarkets. They vary from dehydrated products such as baby rice to jars, packets, tins and cartons of all types of foods. There are strict controls to make sure they do not contain additional sugar, salt or additives. Prepared food products for weaning are sold in tamper-proof or tamper-evident packaging to ensure the hygienic quality of the food product.

Most parents and carers will use prepared baby food products as part of their child's diet

Prepared food products for weaning

Advantages:

+ a wide range of foods are available
+ easy and quick to use
+ the nutritional content is stated on the packet
+ some products have added nutrients
+ the product is safe to eat as it is hygienically prepared and packed
+ products are particularly useful when travelling.

Disadvantages:

+ more expensive than homemade products
+ there may be some wastage if only a small quantity is required
+ some additives are present in some products
+ it is not always possible to tell the amount and proportion of nutrients in all the products.

Key points

+ Babies need to go at their own pace when learning about new tastes and textures.
+ Babies like to feed themselves, which is messy, but it is a stage they need to experience.
+ Babies know when they have eaten enough so they should not be forced to eat more.
+ As much care in food hygiene needs to be taken when preparing weaning foods for baby as when preparing milk feeds.

Key tasks

1 What signs are there to show a baby is ready to start weaning?
2 Explain the stages of weaning.
3 Why should sugar and salt not be added to a baby's food?

Further work

1 Carry out a survey of weaning foods at your local supermarket. Identify the range of products available for each stage of weaning. (RT/IT)
2 Compare the cost and convenience of homemade and prepared weaning foods. (RT/IT)

Diet-related issues

Food refusal

Food refusal is the term used when a child refuses to eat their food. This happens most commonly between the ages of nine months and four years. There are a number of reasons why a child may refuse food:

+ children go through development stages where they will not co-operate with others – it is normal for children to say 'no' and refuse to do something
+ children enjoy mealtimes as an experience and enjoy playing with the food as much as eating it
+ children may not like the taste of the foods they have been given to eat
+ some children have small appetites and do not want or need large quantities of food
+ some young children may see food refusal as a way of seeking attention.

There are many reasons why a young child may refuse food

Parents and carers worry when a toddler refuses to eat. They feel anxious and under pressure to make sure their child eats a nutritionally adequate diet. All children are individuals with there own likes and dislikes, and their tastes change – a food they do not like one day may be eaten the next. When they are hungry they will eat. Very few children become ill because of food refusal. Parents and carers who are concerned can ask for advice from their doctor, health clinic or health visitor.

Medical advice that is given to parents and carers about food refusal by child health centres is:

+ make mealtimes relaxed, social occasions where young children are encouraged but not forced to eat
+ do not give snacks between meals to children who do not eat at mealtimes
+ if your child fails to gain weight as they grow, contact your doctor or health visitor.

Food intolerance

Food intolerance is a reaction to a food or an ingredient in the food product. Food allergy is a type of food intolerance caused by a reaction in the body to a specific food. Food intolerance can produce a wide range of symptoms in babies and young children such as skin rashes, abdominal cramps and more serious reactions. Foods that cause intolerance in babies and young children include milk, wheat, nuts, eggs and fish (see table below).

Foods that can cause intolerance or allergies in babies and young children

Type of intolerance	Foods to avoid
Cow's milk	Cow's milk and milk products such as cream, cheese and butter
Eggs	Eggs and the food products made from eggs such as cakes
Tartrazine	Foods containing tartrazine (E102) or other azo dyes (food colourings)
Gluten	Cereal products containing gluten, such as bread, and other baked products made from wheat, oats, barley or rye
Peanut	Peanuts and food products containing peanut products such as mayonnaise (which contains peanut oil)

It is known that babies who are weaned early are more likely to develop a food intolerance or be allergic to a particular ingredient or food product. It is thought that this is because the baby's body has not yet developed the ability to digest the particular food.

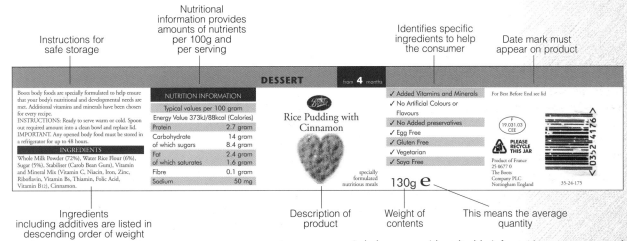

Instructions for safe storage

Nutritional information provides amounts of nutrients per 100g and per serving

Identifies specific ingredients to help the consumer

Date mark must appear on product

DESSERT	from **4** months

Boots body foods are specially formulated to help ensure that your body's nutritional and developmental needs are met. Additional vitamins and minerals have been chosen for every recipe.
INSTRUCTIONS: Ready to serve warm or cold. Spoon out required amount into a clean bowl and replace lid.
IMPORTANT. Any opened body food must be stored in a refrigerator for up to 48 hours.

INGREDIENTS

Whole Milk Powder (72%), Water Rice Flour (6%), Sugar (5%), Stabiliser (Carob Bean Gum), Vitamin and Mineral Mix (Vitamin C, Niacin, Iron, Zinc, Riboflavin, Vitamin B6, Thiamin, Folic Acid, Vitamin B12), Cinnamon.

NUTRITION INFORMATION	
Typical values per 100 gram	
Energy Value 373kJ/88kcal (Calories)	
Protein	2.7 gram
Carbohydrate	14 gram
of which sugars	8.4 gram
Fat	2.4 gram
of which saturates	1.6 gram
Fibre	0.1 gram
Sodium	50 mg

Rice Pudding with Cinnamon

specially formulated nutritious meals

✓ Added Vitamins and Minerals
✓ No Artificial Colours or Flavours
✓ No Added preservatives
✓ Egg Free
✓ Gluten Free
✓ Vegetarian
✓ Soya Free

130g e

For Best Before End see lid

F 19.03.03 CEE

PLEASE RECYCLE THIS JAR

Product of France
25 0677 0
The Boots Company PLC
Nottingham England

35-24-175

Ingredients including additives are listed in descending order of weight

Description of product

Weight of contents

This means the average quantity

Labels can provide valuable information to parents and carers when purchasing food products for children

Young children often grow out of their allergies by the time they start school. Cow's milk intolerance is a common disorder in babies, as it has a different composition to breast milk.

> *Link:* *For more information on breast milk see pages 56–57.*

Coping with a food intolerance

Parents and carers can get specialist help and advice about coping with a food allergy or intolerance from the community dietician. A wide variety of products are available in the supermarket and specialist stores to meet the needs of babies and young children with food allergies and intolerance.

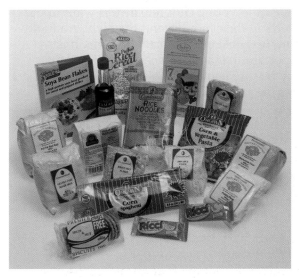

A range of specialist products are available for children with food intolerance

Food labels

Food product labelling has improved, and parents and carers can use the nutritional information on the food label to:

+ identify any particular ingredient that might cause an allergy or intolerance (all ingredients are stated on the product)
+ consider the proportion of nutrient in the product as a percentage of the daily requirement
+ check which ingredients are present in order of weight.

Key points

+ Food intolerance is a reaction to a food or an ingredient in a food product.
+ Foods that commonly cause food intolerance include milk, eggs, nuts and wheat.
+ Specialist products are available for children who have a food intolerance.
+ Labels can give essential information to parents and carers about the content of food products.

Key tasks

1 What advice is given to parents and carers by child health centres about dealing with food refusal?
2 Suggest reasons why children refuse food.
3 Explain what information can be found on a food product label.

Further work Carry out a cost survey of products designed for children with specific food intolerance. (RT/IT)

Food preparation

Food for babies and young children needs to be prepared in a clean and safe environment as they are more vulnerable to infection. Food hygiene is therefore very important and a priority in the baby's first year of life.

Food poisoning

Food products are a source of nutrients for bacteria. If food becomes contaminated with bacteria and is given the correct conditions for growth, the bacteria will multiply rapidly. As bacteria multiply they produce toxins, which are poisons. This is called **food poisoning** or **food borne disease**. Food poisoning is the most common illness in the United Kingdom.

Babies and young children have little resistance to these bacteria and many become seriously ill with gastroenteritis or other similar food-borne diseases.

Gastroenteritis

Every year a number of babies develop this illness. It is more common in bottle-fed babies than in those who are breastfed. This is because there is a greater chance of formula milk being infected during its preparation. Gastroenteritis is an inflammation of the stomach and it is caused by toxins (poisons produced by bacteria). The symptoms of the illness are vomiting and diarrhoea. The baby will become dehydrated very quickly. This is a serious condition in young babies and requires immediate medical help.

How food becomes infected

Food purchased in a supermarket should be safe to eat. Food manufacturers and retailers have to follow strict legal guidelines about the preparation, processing and storage of food – for example ready-made formula feed will be sterile until opened. It is usually after the purchase of the food product that contamination by bacteria occurs.

Bacteria will thrive where they have:

+ warmth – temperatures above 5°C (although very high temperatures destroy bacteria)

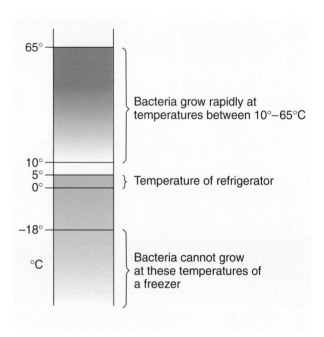

Bacteria grow at temperatures above 5°C

+ foods that they use as a source of nutrients, such as milk, meat and eggs

+ moisture which they need to grow – which is present in most foods.

Food hygiene for young babies

Young babies are vulnerable to food poisoning. Extra care must be taken when preparing bottle foods as milk is an ideal food for bacteria. Babies and young children always want to put objects in their mouths and they will gradually build up resistance to many bacteria. It is important that any surfaces and objects that they use are kept clean to reduce the risks where possible.

Food safety issues include the following:

+ keep food cold to prevent the growth of bacteria – the fridge should be at a constant temperature of between 0 and 5°C
+ keep food covered to prevent cross-contamination
+ the food handler should always keep their hands clean by washing them in between preparing food.

Cross-contamination case study

This case study is an example of cross-contamination where bacteria from one food (the raw chicken) transfers to another (the egg sandwich).

Raw chicken contaminated with salmonella bacteria is prepared on a chopping board before being put in a casserole to cook. The same knife is used to cut and prepare egg sandwiches for a young child's tea. The sandwich is left on a plate in the kitchen for half an hour before tea. The bacteria contaminate the sandwich and grow rapidly in the warm kitchen environment. The child develops the symptoms of food poisoning later that day.

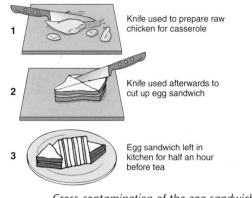

1 Knife used to prepare raw chicken for casserole

2 Knife used afterwards to cut up egg sandwich

3 Egg sandwich left in kitchen for half an hour before tea

Cross-contamination of the egg sandwich

Cross-contamination

Most food naturally contains some bacteria which are not harmful – for example, yoghurt or cheese. Many raw foods, particularly meats, contain bacteria which are destroyed during the cooking process. Foods which are most likely to be contaminated should be stored in a fridge. Other foods should be kept clean by covering it to prevent **cross-contamination**. This is the transfer of bacteria from raw contaminated food to other foods.

Other ways that cross-contamination can occur:

+ hands that are not washed between handling raw and cooked foods
+ liquid from raw meat that drip on other foods in the fridge
+ knives that are used with raw and cooked food without being washed
+ dishcloths used to wipe down food surfaces can spread contamination.

Bacterial infection in the home

Family pets should not be allowed in the food preparation areas, as they can carry and transfer bacteria to surfaces. Flies can contaminate food by transferring bacteria from one source to another, for example from a dustbin outside to a child's feeder mug. People with coughs and colds can transfer infection to food by coughing or sneezing over it.

Link: *For more information on infections see pages 66–67.*

For further reference

The Food Safety (General Food Hygiene) Regulations (1995) control the hygienic practices for food manufacturers and retailers.

The Food Safety (Temperature Control) Regulations (1995) states the necessary temperatures for the storage of food in retail outlets.

For more information on food safety visit the Department of Health website at www.doh.gov.uk/safety.html

Key points

+ Careful storage of food can reduce the risk of food poisoning.
+ Cross-contamination of food is the transfer of bacteria from raw contaminated foods to other foods.
+ Babies and young children are vulnerable to food poisoning.

Key tasks

1 List and explain the different ways that cross-contamination of food can occur.
2 Explain why food hygiene is so important for young babies.
3 What conditions do food poisoning bacteria need to grow?

Further work Design a simple poster for the local clinic to explain the dangers of poor food hygiene when preparing food. (RT/IT)

Response to infection

How disease spreads

As children grow they are likely to suffer from one or more **infectious diseases**. Infectious diseases are caused by bacteria or viruses and are spread by:

+ contact
+ droplet infection.

Diseases such as chickenpox are spread by contact. They are sometimes called contagious diseases. The contact can be by touching the infected child or by touching articles such as toys used by the child. Droplet infection occurs when tiny drops of moisture containing bacteria or viruses spread from the nose or throat of an infected person when they cough or sneeze.

Incubation period

When the child is infected the bacteria or virus will multiply and grow. The **incubation period** is the time between catching the illness and the appearance of the first **symptoms** of the disease. Symptoms are the changes in the child's body which show the disease, such as spots.

Infectious stage

At this stage the bacteria can spread from the child with the infection to others. The infectious stage usually happens towards the end of the incubation period and for up to a week after the symptoms first appear.

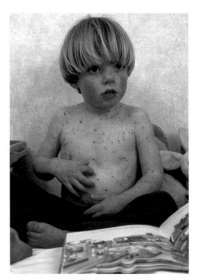

These spots are a symptom of chickenpox

Children are infectious before they develop the symptoms of the disease themselves. By the time the symptoms are evident they may have infected other children. This is why childhood diseases spread rapidly (see table below).

Parental responsibility

A chart or reference book can help parents and carers identify the symptoms of an infectious disease. If a child develops an infectious disease they should inform:

Common infectious childhood diseases

Disease	Incubation period	Symptoms	Treatment
Chickenpox	11–21 days	Child feels unwell. Slight rise in temperature. Rash appears in 24 hours with red raised spots that blister and form crusts	Treat spots with calamine lotion to stop itching. Give plenty to drink and paracetamol to lower the temperature. Keep child in bed and away from pregnant women
Mumps	14–21 days	A slight fever and sore throat, with swelling on one or both sides of the jaw up to the ear. The child may have difficulty in chewing and swallowing	Give plenty to drink (but not fruit juices) and paracetamol to reduce pain. Keep child in bed
Rubella (German measles)	14–21 days	Slight rise in temperature followed by a rash of flat, pink spots on the face and body. Swollen glands in the neck are often present	Give plenty to drink, and keep them away from pregnant women
Whooping cough (pertussis)	7–14 days	Begins like a cold and cough, which gradually gets worse. Sometimes develops into a whooping noise. Coughing bouts that make it difficult to breathe and may caue the child to choke and vomit	Antibiotics are often prescribed for this disease. The child needs plenty of rest and fluids. It will take a few weeks to recover from this illness
Measles	7–12 days	Begins like a bad cold and cough. Child becomes more unwell, with a temperature and sore, watery eyes. Rash appears with dark, blotchy (but not itchy) red spots on the face and neck and then on the rest of the body	Measles can be a severe illness and the child will need careful nursing until their temperature drops. The room should be kept quiet and dark. Give plenty to drink and paracetamol to lower the temperature

✦ their GP, who will treat the illness
✦ any playgroups, nursery, childminder or school the child attends
✦ parents and carers of other children with whom the child has been in recent contact.

Most playgroups, nurseries and childminders have policies on whether they accept children when they are ill.

Other infectious diseases

✦ Meningitis. This is a very serious childhood infection caused by a bacteria or virus. It is the inflammation of the meninges, which is part of the brain and nervous systems. Symptoms of the disease may include blotchy skin, fever and stiffness of the neck. A doctor will take immediate action if he or she suspects a child has the symptoms of meningitis, as it is an infection that develops very rapidly.
✦ Coughs and colds. All children develop coughs and colds at some time. They are spread by droplet infection. Children are most likely to catch colds when they first start playgroup or school and mix with a larger numbers of children.

Common childhood ailments

Children can develop other forms of illness, which are not infectious. Common ailments of young babies include:

✦ colic. The baby will be uncomfortable and in pain because of a build up of wind in the stomach. Winding a baby during feeding can help avoid colic. Simple remedies such as gripe water are available for colic. If the symptoms are severe a doctor may prescribe drugs.
✦ cradle cap. The baby develops a layer of scurf on the scalp. This is harmless and can be removed by softening with baby oil.
✦ vomiting. Most babies vomit a small amount during and after feeding. If the vomiting is more severe, often called 'projectile', it can be a symptom of a more serious illness and a doctor should be consulted. Projectile vomiting causes the baby to dehydrate. It can be a symptom of food poisoning or gastroenteritis.

Other childhood ailments include:

✦ asthma. There is an increase in the number of children suffering from asthma today. Asthma can be triggered by allergic reaction or by an infection. Doctors prescribe treatment for asthma.
✦ earache. Many children develop earache as a side effect of a cold or cough. This may develop into an inflammation of the inner ear and can be very painful for the child. Severe earache needs treatment from a doctor.

For further reference

For more information on childhood ailments and diseases visit the NHS Direct Online website at www.nhsdirect.nhs.uk

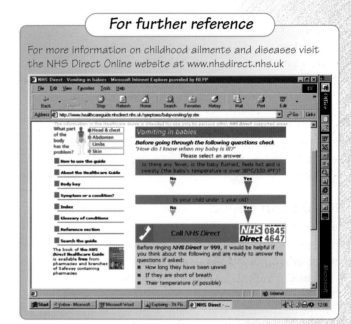

Key points

✦ Infectious diseases are spread by contact and droplet infection.
✦ The incubation period is the time between the first contact with the bacteria and the first symptoms of the disease.
✦ If a child develops an infectious disease the parents and carers should contact their GP.

Key tasks

1 How are infectious diseases spread?
2 Describe the symptoms of chickenpox and explain the treatment that parents and carers can give to the child.
3 Explain why it is important for parents and carers to inform the playgroup or nursery if their child has an infectious disease.

Immunization

Immunity is the body's ability to resist infection. Immunity can be given to a child by **immunization**. Children are given a **vaccine** that makes their bodies produce antibodies to fight infection. Immunization is sometimes also called vaccination.

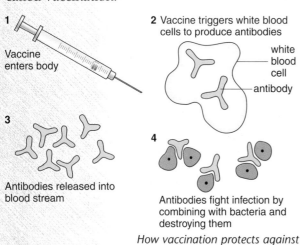

1 Vaccine enters body

2 Vaccine triggers white blood cells to produce antibodies

white blood cell
antibody

3 Antibodies released into blood stream

4 Antibodies fight infection by combining with bacteria and destroying them

How vaccination protects against infectious diseases

Having children immunized gives extra protection against some very serious illnesses. The local child health clinic or GP arranges for immunizations to take place. This has resulted in many diseases like polio and diphtheria being rare in the United Kingdom. Having babies and children immunized at an early age means they are protected against disease by the time they start playgroup and come into contact with lots of other children.

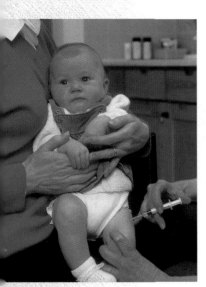

It is important to have babies immunized at an early age

Immunization programme

The immunization programme is part of the National Health Service provision.

Health centres provide parents and carers with an immunization record card to note down when their child is immunized. The record is also kept on a central database at the health centre or GP's surgery, so parents and carers can be told the date to bring in the child for the vaccine. The table below shows the current immunization programme that is recommended for children.

Immunization programme

When it is given	Immunization	How it is given
8 weeks	Polio	By mouth
	Diphtheria	One injection
	Tetanus	
	Pertussis (whooping cough)	
	Hib	
	Meningitis C	
12 weeks	Polio	By mouth
	Diphtheria	One injection
	Tetanus	
	Pertussis (whooping cough)	
	Hib	
	Meningitis C	
16 weeks	Polio	By mouth
	Diphtheria	One injection
	Tetanus	
	Pertussis (whooping cough)	
	Hib	
	Meningitis C	
12–15 months	Measles ⎫	One injection
	Mumps ⎬ (MMR)	
	Rubella ⎭	
	Meningitis C	
3–5 years	Polio	By mouth
	Diphtheria	One injection
	Tetanus	
	Measles ⎫	
	Mumps ⎬ (MMR)	
	Rubella ⎭	

Types of immunization

The DTP-Hib ('triple') vaccine is given to a child at eight, twelve and sixteen weeks. It protects against diphtheria, tetanus and pertussis (whooping cough) and also against an infection called haemophilus influenzae type B (Hib). Tetanus bacteria are found in the soil and enter the body through a cut – it is a painful disease that affects the muscles and can cause paralysis. A diphtheria and tetanus booster is given at three to five years (usually before the child starts school). Hib is an infection that can cause serious illnesses including pneumonia and meningitis.

Polio is a virus that attacks the nervous system and can cause permanent muscle paralysis. The immunization programme has meant that polio no longer occurs in the United Kingdom but it is still common in other parts of the world. The polio vaccine is taken by mouth when the child is two, three and four months old. A booster is given at three to five years.

In 1999 there were over 1500 cases of meningitis C. This disease is the commonest cause of death in children aged between one and five years. A new vaccine has been developed to protect against meningitis C and this is now given to babies as part of the immunization programme with the DTP-Hib vaccine.

The MMR vaccine is given to children between twelve and fifteen months of age. It protects against measles, mumps and Rubella (German measles). Before the vaccine was introduced, about 90 children a year used to die in the United Kingdom from measles. Some children have a mild reaction to the MMR vaccine and become feverish, develop a mild rash and go off their food for two or three days.

Importance of immunization

Before birth, antibodies cross the placenta from the mother's blood to the baby's blood. The baby is therefore born with the same immunity to infection as the mother. If the baby is breastfed it continues to receive antibodies in the milk. As the baby grows it starts to develop his or her own immune system. At this time he or she needs the extra protection against illnesses that can be given by immunization.

Contra-indications

Some parents and carers worry about their child's reaction to a vaccine. If they have reacted badly to a previous vaccine this is called a **contra-indication**. Parents and carers can discuss this with their GP at their child health

clinic. For a very small number of children, there is a risk from side effects of the vaccine.

Should children be immunized?

Some parents and carers wonder if they should immunize their children against diseases that are no longer common, such as polio and diphtheria. However, these diseases have been overcome because of the immunization programme – if children are not immunized these diseases will become common again. Immunization is important because:

+ every child immunized reduces the risk to other children
+ there is much more risk to health from the diseases than from the vaccine.

There are very few reasons why a child should not be immunized. Parents and carers should let the doctor or health visitor know if their child has a high fever, has had convulsions or fits or has reacted badly to previous vaccines.

Key points

+ Immunization protects the body against infections.
+ The National Health Service provides an immunization programme for children.
+ Immunization has made sure that diseases which were once common, such as diphtheria and polio, are now rare.
+ A contra-indication is a reaction to a previous vaccine.

Key tasks

1 Explain how a vaccine can prevent infectious diseases.
2 Why is it important that children are immunized before they start playgroup?
3 Why might some parents and carers not want their child to be immunized?
4 What does the term contra-indication mean?

Further work

Visit your local health centre or primary care practice and see what information is available about immunization programmes for children. (RT/IT)

Caring for sick children (1)

Every child will get ill at some time in his or her childhood. When a normally lively child looks listless and unwell it is a time of anxiety for his or her parents and carers. Most childhood illnesses pass quickly and help the child build up immunity to disease.

Every child will get ill at some time

How to tell if a child is unwell

When babies and young children are unwell they need to be cared for. Usually it is easy to tell if a child is ill by their behaviour, which changes when they are becoming ill. Other signs that a child is ill include:

✦ loss of appetite
✦ flushed appearance
✦ raised temperature
✦ being irritable and clinging
✦ tiredness
✦ crying.

Young babies cannot explain that they feel ill and they can develop infections rapidly. The following symptoms in a child should prompt a parent or carer to get help immediately:

✦ a fit, or if the child turns blue or very pale
✦ a very high temperature (over 39°C), especially with a rash

✦ difficulty in breathing
✦ unusually sleepy or hard to wake up
✦ a purple-red rash anywhere on the body, as this could be a sign of meningitis.

Taking temperature

Body temperature is a reliable sign that the child may be unwell. A child's temperature can vary anywhere between 36.5°C and 37.5°C. Parents and carers will need to take a young child's temperature as one way of finding out if the child is ill. There are several different types of thermometer available (see table below).

Types of thermometer

Type of thermometer	Description
Clinical	A thin tube of glass with a bulb, usually containing mercury, at one end. When warmed the mercury expands and rises in the tube to display temperature reading
	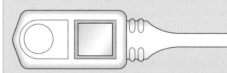
Digital	Digital thermometers are more expensive but easier to use. The heat of the body is read through a sensor and is given as a digital reading. Ear digital thermometers take the temperature in one second
Strip-type	These are usually not as reliable as digital and clinical thermometers (as they show the skin and not the body temperature), but they are very easy to use and do give an indication of temperature change. The heat-sensitive strip is placed against a baby's or child's forehead and the body heat changes the colour of the strip to give a reading
	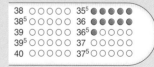

Taking a child's temperature

1. Make sure the thermometer is clean. Shake down the mercury to below the arrow for a normal temperature.
2. Tuck the thermometer into the child's armpit and hold his or her arm against their body. An older child of five years or more could have the thermometer placed under the tongue.
   Leave the thermometer there for at least five minutes to let the mercury register the correct temperature.
3. Remove the thermometer and read carefully from the scale.
4. Wash the thermometer (but don't use hot water) and store safely.

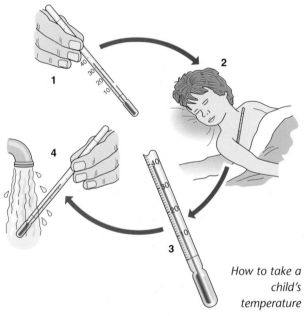

How to take a child's temperature

A low temperature can be just as serious as a high temperature, as it can be an indication of hypothermia. Hypothermia is where the temperature of the whole body drops very low so the baby or young child gets extremely cold. Hypothermia is a serious condition and medical help needs to be given.

Children's medicine

It is usually best to consult a doctor before giving medicines to a baby or child. Most children's medicines are given in the form of syrup, often sugar free. If they are given in tablet form they must be crushed before they are given to the child. The following gives guidelines for giving medicines to a child:

+ read the instructions on the packet carefully
+ make sure the instructions are followed closely about the timing and dosage of the medicine
+ unless instructed otherwise, complete the course of the medication even if the child appears to have recovered
+ store medicines in a safe place, out of reach and locked away from children, to avoid accidental poisoning
+ throw away old medicines – out-of-date medicines are not effective.

When to call a doctor

Parents and carers are usually are the best judges of when the child is unwell. They will know when they need to contact the doctor. Most doctor's surgeries will allow the parent or carer to speak to the doctor on the phone if the doctor is not available immediately. Parents and carers need to be able to give the doctor the following information:

+ the symptoms the child has
+ how long they have had these symptoms
+ the child's temperature and whether it is continuing to rise
+ the length of time the child has had the high temperature.

Key points

+ All children become ill at some point in their childhood.
+ A high temperature is a reliable sign that a child is unwell.
+ Doctors should be consulted before giving medicine to children.

Key tasks

1 How can you tell if a baby or child is unwell?
2 Describe how to take the temperature of a toddler.
3 Explain the guidelines for giving medicine to a child.

| **Further work** | Carry out a survey to find out how parents and carers take their child's temperature. (RT) |

Caring for sick children (2)

A sick child needs:

+ rest and sleep in a quiet room
+ medication prescribed by the doctor
+ plenty of fluids to drink
+ a warm and draught-free room at about 22°C
+ comfort and reassurance from the family.

When a child is ill, he or she will need a lot more attention and care. When they are awake they may want the company of others for reassurance. Left alone they may be fretful and demanding. Special toys and games can be used to try and occupy the child. How much activity they can cope with will depend on the stage of the illness. When children are unwell they will want activities they can watch rather than actively participate in, such as having stories read, watching television, listening to tapes and looking at books. When they are getting better they will enjoy participating more with jigsaws, crayoning books or construction toys, depending on the age of the child. The best place for a sick child is at home in his or her own bed, where he or she feel secure.

A child feels secure at home in bed

Hospital

Sometimes babies and young children need to go to hospital. Up to 40 per cent of all children under the age of five have a hospital stay during their early childhood. The main reasons young children stay in hospital include:

+ accidents that have caused injury such as broken bones or burns
+ infections of the chest or stomach
+ surgery for medical conditions
+ medical care for congenital conditions.

A hospital stay is a difficult experience for the child. He or she is in different surroundings with a strange routine and different food. Most hospitals work together with the parents and carers to help the child settle in. Support systems to enable parents and carers to stay with their children are often available. The need of parents or carers to be with their child is recognized by the Department of Health. Parents and carers should be able to be with their child whenever they like. Recommendations are that:

+ there is unlimited visiting for parents and carers of children in hospital
+ provision is made for parents and carers to stay overnight with very young children whenever possible.

For further reference

An organization that supports the improvement of facilities for parents and carers is the Action For Sick Children. Their website is www.actionforsickchildren.org.uk

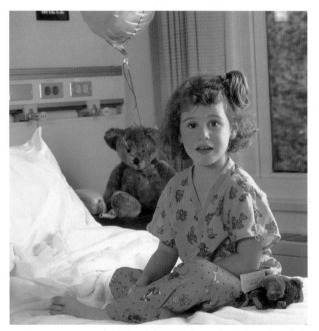

Up to 40 per cent of children under five have a hospital stay

Preparing a child for a stay in hospital

It is important that a child is prepared for a hospital stay as it may be the first time he or she has been away from home and family. Hospitals can be frightening places for children so it is a good idea to prepare them for the stay:

+ talk about what will happen in hospital – the more you explain the better he or she will cope with the situation
+ explain about the jobs of nurses and other hospital staff
+ show the child books and tell them stories about being in hospital
+ encourage role-play games about hospitals
+ try to visit the hospital with the child beforehand and talk to staff about anything that will be important for your child such as particular likes and dislikes
+ let the child pack their own suitcase to help them feel they are part of the process. Make sure they pack their favourite things such as teddy bears.

The child can help pack their suitcase

Returning home from hospital

When the child returns home from hospital it will probably take him or her a while to settle back to the old routine. It is normal for children to become clinging or attention seeking afterwards. Reassurance and affection will help the child adjust back to their normal routine quite quickly.

Regression

Any form of illness can affect a child's developmental progress. A severe or prolonged illness can actually cause the child to **regress**. Regression is when a child returns to behaviour they showed when they were younger. For example, a four-year-old who has had a prolonged hospital stay could start to have tantrums. When the child returns to normal health, he or she will soon start to make progress again.

Key points

+ A sick child will need more attention and care than normal.
+ The best place for a sick child is at home in bed where he or she feels secure.
+ Hospital stays are difficult for children, and parents and carers should be able to be with their child as much as is possible.
+ After a hospital stay children may find it difficult to adjust back to their routine.

Key tasks

1 Describe how to prepare a three-year-old child for a hospital stay.
2 Explain the needs of a sick child.
3 Why might a child regress after a prolonged stay in hospital?

Further work

1 Find out what facilities are available at your local hospital for parents and carers of young children. (RT/IT)
2 Complete a table like the one below to identify the toys and activities that would be suitable to amuse a sick child.

Age of child	Toy or activity	Reasons for choice
12 months		
2½ years		
4 years		

Conditions for intellectual development

Intellectual development is the development of the mind. It is also known as **cognitive** development and is about the child's understanding, reasoning and learning. Intellectual development depends on two main factors:

+ the genes the child has inherited
+ the environment the child is brought up in.

The term '**nature** and **nurture**' is often used for describing these factors. Nature refers to the child's natural ability inherited from his or her parents and nurture refers to the way the child is stimulated and the amount of interaction that takes place with those around the child.

As with other areas of development, a child develops at his or her own pace, but the amount of stimulation and encouragement that a child receives will affect the learning process. Conditions for the child to develop to their full potential include an environment where:

+ people talk and communicate
+ the child is offered visual stimulation, e.g. pictures, mobiles, toys to look at
+ the child is given love and security
+ the child is given a healthy diet.

In these conditions the child will develop the following skills:

+ concentration
+ memory
+ language
+ creativity
+ imagination
+ the building up of **concepts** (ideas).

The senses

The senses play an important part in a child's learning process. Children use all five senses – sight, smell, taste, touch and hearing – in order to develop. Parents or carers can encourage and stimulate the child's senses by providing mobiles, a variety of toys and objects and by putting the child in positions where they can see what is going on around them.

Children learn by building one skill into another. For example, textures are important to young babies who enjoy the feel of different objects, whereas older babies will enjoy objects that can move around or make a noise. This is an example of a pattern of learning.

How children learn

Children learn using a number of different factors.

Exploring

Children learn by exploring whatever is around them. When babies become mobile they should be offered toys and objects that are interesting, and the child will therefore gain information and knowledge. The greater the variety of objects, the more information the child will learn.

Babies learn by studying objects around them

Repetition

Children learn by listening to and looking at what is going on. If this is repeated time and time again (e.g. as in a nursery rhyme), they will soon learn and remember what is being said or what is happening. Memories are built up in this way. A memory will be used for storing and recalling information that can be used at a later date.

Imitation

Children develop intellectual skills by copying what they see and hear in their environment. A child will learn new sounds, words and right from wrong by copying the people around them. Role-play – when children copy adult roles – is an important part of this learning process, e.g. dressing up games, playing mummies and daddies or doctors and nurses.

Looking at books

Children learn by sharing a book with an adult. Picture books, books that make sounds or contain different textures are important for young babies. Older children will have books that include printed words, but pictures are still important. Reading stories to children will help with listening skills, concentration and vocabulary.

Sharing a book

Asking questions

When a child can talk, he or she will ask constant questions and these should be answered so that the child gains knowledge. Parents or carers must be patient and give answers that are clear.

WHY? WHERE? WHEN? HOW?

At around three years children will ask constant questions

Understanding concepts

Concepts are learnt as the child gains knowledge from playing and finding out about the world around him or her. Children begin to understand concepts such as heat, light and time as part of the learning process.

Parents and carers

Parents and carers have important roles to play in helping a child's intellectual development. Adults should:

- ✦ provide stimulation
- ✦ provide encouragement
- ✦ provide support
- ✦ provide opportunities to play
- ✦ explain information
- ✦ help the child to remember.

Pre-school

Pre-school groups also are important for a child's early education. They build on the child's learning and offer a variety of stimulating activities in order for the intellectual development to progress.

Key points

- ✦ A child's intellectual development is dependent upon the genes inherited from the parents and the environment that the child is growing up in.
- ✦ Children learn by exploring their senses, by repetition, by imitation, by looking at books and by asking questions.
- ✦ Adults around the child can provide learning opportunities for the progression of intellectual development.

Key tasks

1 What are the two main factors that intellectual development depends on?
2 How can a parent or carer provide the stimulation of a child's senses?
3 How does a child learn through imitation?
4 What part can a parent or carer play in helping a child's intellectual development?

Further work

1 Design and make a simple book to encourage a child's awareness of time. (RT)
2 Observe a child's intellectual skills by setting up an activity involving colour recognition. (IT)

Stages of intellectual development

As with all areas of development, intellectual development has **milestones** that show the average age at which a child progresses. It must be remembered that the ages given below are only average ages, as each child is different and will develop at his or her own rate.

+ newborn babies explore using their senses – sight, touch, hearing, smell and taste
+ at one month, a baby will recognize their parent or carer
+ at three months, a baby will play with their hands, take an interest in the surroundings and grasp objects
+ by six months, a baby will want to be involved in an activity and will understand objects, e.g. if it is a musical toy the child will expect it to play music. The child will also show some understanding of the parent's or carer's voice, e.g. if the parent or carer is laughing
+ at around nine months, babies can look in the direction of fallen toys, recognize familiar pictures, understand simple instructions and play 'not there' games, e.g. hide a toy and then look for it
+ by twelve months, the baby can copy actions and treat objects in a relevant way, e.g. use a hairbrush correctly
+ at fifteen months, babies can remember people, recognize and sort shapes and understand the names of various parts of the body
+ by eighteen months, toddlers can recognize themselves in a photograph, begin to develop a memory for places and obey simple instructions
+ at two years, the child can begin to understand the consequences of their actions, e.g. if they drop an object they know it may break, and they can do simple jigsaw puzzles.
+ at two and a half years, the child will constantly ask questions, know their full name and notice details in pictures
+ by around three years, the child will understand the concept of time, remember songs and nursery rhymes, recognize colours and compare sizes of objects
+ by four years, the child can count up to twenty, has developed memory skills, can solve simple problems, draw people and sort objects into groups
+ at around five years, the child can produce detailed drawings, will act out adult roles with friends or alone, can understand past, present and future tenses and show an interest in reading and writing.

Mathematical concepts

Understanding numbers

The understanding of numbers is a gradual process for a child. Numbers regularly occur in conversation and in songs and stories, so the child will become aware of numbers in the every day world around them. At around the age of two to three years, children can repeat numbers but do not understand what they mean. After this stage, children will learn how to match numbers with objects and then that numbers have an order.

Understanding size/mass and volume

This is also a gradual but important process in the development of a child's mathematical concepts. Providing the child is encouraged with a variety of activities, he or she will begin to recognize and compare size at an early age.

Bath toys and toys used in a sandpit, e.g. beakers and buckets, will encourage filling and emptying containers to help develop these concepts. Scales and stacking beakers will also help. Pre-school education also offers a variety of facilities to help encourage these concepts in a child's intellectual development.

Learning to draw

All children love to draw, and providing they are encouraged and given materials, e.g. pencils, crayons and paper, a child will draw and create pictures of the world around them. Drawing encourages fine manipulative skills as well as intellectual development. At around one year, if a child is shown how to hold a pencil, he or she will start to draw. A child can develop their imagination and express their feelings through drawing.

There are several stages of drawing, and many of these overlap, but there is a pattern of how children develop these skills. The first stages of drawing are a series of scribbles, and the control of the pencil or crayon is dependent on the child's manipulative skills.

The child produces scribbles by the hand moving backwards and forwards

The crayon can be lifted from the paper and it is moved in different directions

The child scribbles in circles

The child can draw circles

A circle is drawn with details of the nose, mouth and eyes

The child adds lines around the circle

The lines are arranged to represent the arms and legs

The child draws two circles to represent the head and the body. The arms are drawn coming out of the head

The legs have feet and the body is now important

Drawings are more detailed and include everyday items from the child's life, e.g. houses and trees.

Key points

+ A child gradually understands a variety of things such as names and body parts.
+ The parent or carer needs to provide stimulation to encourage a child to go through these milestones:
+ Mathematical concepts will be understood by a child who is provided with numbers in conversation and in everyday life.

Key tasks

1 Give the average age for the following intellectual milestones:
   a Recognizing familiar pictures.
   b Remembering people.
   c Constantly asking questions.
   d Producing detailed drawings.
2 How can a parent or carer encourage a child to develop mathematical concepts?
3 What skills does drawing encourage?

Further work

1 Design and make a simple card game to encourage a young child to count. (RT)
2 Observe a child's drawing skills and record their level of development. Use the drawing made by the child as evidence. (IT)

The development of language

The development of language and communication begins after birth. Babies are born with a need to communicate with other people before they can speak. They learn non-verbal messages from their parents and others around them. This is known as **non-verbal communication**. Babies communicate with others by:

+ making noises
+ using facial expressions
+ making eye contact
+ using their hands by pointing, touching and pulling at objects.

Babies start to learn to talk – **verbal communication** – very early. Children who are spoken to, or are in an environment where there is a lot of speech activity or stimulation, will develop language skills more quickly than those who are not stimulated with speech. As with all areas of development, children develop at their own pace, but there are reasons for some of these variations of pace:

+ boys tend to talk later than girls
+ the baby may be concentrating on another aspect of development, e.g. walking
+ an older brother or sister may 'talk' for the baby, so he or she may not need to talk
+ there is a lack of stimulation from the family
+ a hearing problem will cause the baby to miss the important stages in learning to speak.

Stages of language development (communication)

There are milestones in communication development that children pass through, and these are the average ages:

+ newborn babies communicate by moving their legs and arms when responding to high-pitched tones, making eye contact and crying to show they are hungry
+ at one month, the baby may make noises, e.g. gurgle, will respond to an adult by looking at them and will interact by cooing when spoken to
+ at three months, the baby will smile, exchange noises with a familiar person and cry loudly.

A smiling baby is communicating with others

+ at six months, the baby can make four sounds, e.g. 'goo', 'der', 'adah', and 'ka', looks for the source of sounds and will talk to themselves in a tuneful voice
+ at around nine months, the baby may say words like 'dad-dad' and 'mum-mum', and will imitate sounds, e.g. a cough
+ by twelve months, the baby will be able to follow simple instructions and can say 'bye bye'
+ at around fifteen months, the baby can join in with nursery rhymes and songs and respond to simple commands

Children at twelve months can wave bye bye

+ by eighteen months, the toddler will babble sentences, say six or more words and respond to simple questions
+ at around two years, the child can form two-word sentences, understand many more words than he or she can speak, and will constantly name everyday objects
+ by two and a half years, the child can use questions and pronouns, e.g. I, you, me, and say some rhymes and songs
+ at around three years, a child can form three- to four-word sentences, tell stories, carry on simple conversations, have a vocabulary of up to 200 words, and will learn more than one language if they live in a bilingual family
+ by four years old, the child can give descriptions of events that have taken place, match words with pictures, talk fluently, say his or her full name and address and enjoy jokes
+ at five years, the child is fluent and grammatically correct in his or her speech, and shows an interest in language, reading and writing.

How a child learns verbal communication

The baby learns to talk by making sounds and then learning to put them in order. He or she can be helped to do this by:

+ other people, especially adults, talking to the baby
+ listening to sounds, e.g. music, voices and singing
+ practising sounds him/herself
+ copying sounds made by others.

If sounds are not made around the baby or child, he or she will not learn to speak very well. Babies and children need to be stimulated by parents or carers in order to develop their language. Interaction (talking with others, having conversations) with adults is an important part of a child's speech and vocabulary development. Adults can help by:

+ listening to the child
+ being patient
+ talking directly to the child
+ repeating words and phrases
+ praising and encouraging the child
+ answering questions
+ reading stories
+ singing nursery rhymes.

Key points

+ Babies can communicate in a non-verbal way with other people.
+ They learn language at an early age and, provided they are given stimulation with speech, they will develop through the milestones of communication with few problems.
+ The rate of development may vary from child to child for a variety of reasons.
+ Children who are not given any stimulation may have speech difficulties.

Key tasks

1 Give four ways a baby can communicate before they can speak.
2 Suggest three reasons why a child may be slow in their language development.
3 Give an average age for the following communication milestones:
  a Smiling.
  b Saying 'mum-mum'.
  c Responding to simple questions.
  d Forming three- to four-word sentences.
  e Saying his or her full name and address.
4 How can a child be helped to learn verbal communication?
5 Explain how adults can encourage a child's speech development.

Further work

1 Design and make a matching picture and word game that would encourage a child's speech development. (RT)
2 Set up an activity with a child that involves singing nursery rhymes. Record the activity on a cassette tape and write up your findings. (IT)

Speech problems and pre-reading skills

Speech problems

Sometimes children may have problems in learning to speak. Children will only learn to speak if they can hear others speaking around them. They need to be stimulated by sounds and speech if progression in language development is to be made. It is natural for young children to make mistakes when they are learning to pronounce words, and these usually disappear by the time the child is five years old. Some common **mispronunciations** are:

+ 'yeth' instead of 'yes'
+ 'lellow' instead of 'yellow'
+ 'fevver' instead of 'feather'.

Stammering

Stammering (or stuttering) is another common problem that young children may experience when learning to speak. This usually occurs between the ages of two to four years. Children tend to speak so quickly that they make mistakes and stammer over the words. This is a normal stage that most children go through. Adults should not put pressure on the child to speak correctly as this may make the problem worse. Instead, adults should be patient and give praise and encouragement to a child who is stammering. If, however, the problem continues beyond the age of four or when the child starts school, help may be needed from a speech therapist. A speech therapist specializes in speech problems and is trained to help children to correct their speech.

Deafness

Deafness is linked to poor speech development. It is very important for a child to have regular hearing tests so that any problems with hearing can be identified and treated. A deaf child will be slow to learn to speak, or may not be able to speak at all if the deafness is total.

Pre-reading skills

Pre-reading is a term used to describe all the skills a child needs to have acquired before learning to read. Reading is linked to language development, since it encourages and increases the child's vocabulary and grammar. Pre-reading skills include:

+ being able to match similar objects together, e.g. dominoes, pictures and shape sorting
+ playing games, e.g. snakes and ladders or ludo, that involve counting
+ knowing that symbols represent something, e.g. green traffic light means go
+ understanding the sequence of events, e.g. in a story.

Sorting shapes

Books

Babies and young children can be encouraged to develop pre-reading skills by parents or carers providing books from an early age. First books should have large, colourful pictures of everyday objects to attract the baby's attention. They are usually made of cloth or thick board, as the baby will put them into his or her mouth and suck them. Books that are waterproof and made of plastic can be used in the bath.

Exploring a picture book

Pre-writing skills

Before starting school, it will help if the child has acquired some pre-writing skills. These are closely linked to speech development as well as pre-reading skills. It is useful for the child to be able to hold a pencil correctly, and perhaps to be able to form shapes of letters. Reading books will help develop skills such as learning to spell and using grammar and punctuation correctly. All these skills will develop gradually once the child has started school, and parents and carers should continue to encourage him or her.

Key points

✦ Speech problems are common, and most children pass through this stage without too much difficulty.

✦ Pre-reading activities are very important to prepare a child for learning to read.

✦ Parents or carers should offer stimulation by providing a variety of books, and by reading stories to their children.

Key tasks

1 a At around what age does stammering occur?

b How can a parent or carer help a child who is stammering?

2 Why is it important that deafness is identified in a young child?

3 a Suggest three pre-reading skills.

b Explain how a parent or carer can encourage these skills.

Further work

1 Investigate the wide variety of books that are available for children under the age of five. Record your findings in an appropriate way, making use of ICT. (RT)

2 Prepare an activity that could be used with a child to encourage a pre-reading skill. Carry out the activity as an observation. (IT)

Alphabet or number books are appropriate for a child aged twelve months and older. These will encourage the development of number and letter recognition. Nursery rhyme or song books will encourage a child to join in and learn these rhymes.

'Lift the flap' books, and books that make noises when buttons are pressed, add to the variety of items available. These will add interest and stimulation for the child.

Children of all ages enjoy being read to, and parents or carers should include a story in the child's regular bedtime routine to encourage reading as an enjoyable activity when the child gets older.

From around the age of three years, the child will spend a long time looking at books. By now, these books will contain simple stories and a child will know these stories well. At this age, a child's concentration will start to increase and they will be able to tell a story by looking at the pictures.

All these pre-reading skills will help a child when they start school and begin to read for themselves. Children should still be read aloud to, and should be continually stimulated by their parents or carers to read. A variety of books should always be available so that the child can select a book for pleasure. Visits to the local library could also be made, especially if there are not many books at home.

Learning through play

All children play, and this is a natural way of learning and discovering about everything around them. Play is important as it encourages all the areas of development – social, physical, intellectual, emotional and language. There are several different types of play:

+ physical
+ creative
+ imaginative
+ exploratory
+ manipulative
+ social.

Physical play

This type of play encourages the development of **gross motor skills** and **fine manipulative skills**.

Physical play is to do with physical activities, e.g. running, climbing, playing with a ball, and helps the child with body co-ordination.

Creative play

Creative play is to do with a child expressing his or her feelings through playing with a variety of materials. Play with dough, painting, colouring, making music, and building/construction toys

are all examples of types of creative play. This type of play encourages the development of physical and intellectual skills.

Imaginative play

By the age of two years, a child has begun to develop an imagination. It is at this age that imaginative play becomes part of a child's learning process. **Role-play** or 'pretend play' becomes important to children, as it helps them to understand how people behave and the world around them. A box of dressing up clothes for the child to use encourages pretend play, and the child can act out adult roles, e.g. as doctors and nurses, teachers and so on. By expressing themselves in this way, the child is progressing his or her emotional development.

Providing items such as cardboard boxes allows a child to develop its imagination, as he or she may use it as a lorry or car. Reading stories and listening to story tapes will also develop the imagination.

Exploratory play

Exploratory play involves the senses of sight, touch, smell taste and hearing – this is known as **sensory exploration**. Babies explore their fingers to begin with, and then any object that they can reach. All the senses are used as these objects are held, sucked, smelt, looked at and, if they make a noise, listened to. Sensory exploration is developed further by the older child, who will use all the senses in a more refined way when playing. For example, touch and sight are used to explore a variety of textures when using dressing up clothes, or smell and taste are used when cutting out dough to make cookies.

Exploratory play enables a child to find things out for itself when he or she is ready and at his or her own pace. Sand and water, along with different-sized beakers, are excellent materials for the child to learn and develop mathematical/scientific concepts. Shapes, colours, textures, weight and volume are also learnt through exploratory play.

Manipulative play

Manipulative play is to do with the movement of the hands. This encourages physical development and **hand–eye co-ordination**. Babies play with rattles, activity centres, and so on. For the older child, sewing cards, threading beads, dot-to-dot and drawing are all activities that stimulate manipulative play.

Social play

Social play is to do with the way children play together. This type of play encourages the social development of a child. Sharing and being co-operative within a group teaches acceptable social behaviour.

Link: *For more information on social development see pages 86–89.*

Linking the types of play

All these types of play are linked together. During a play activity, the child may be using more than one type, e.g. playing a game of pirates with a group of children will involve social, imaginative and physical play.

Apart from encouraging the development areas, play also:

* prevents boredom
* reduces stress
* diverts aggression
* helps towards happiness
* helps children to find out about the world around them.

Key points

✦ Play is very important to all children so that they can learn and gain information.
✦ Play helps stimulate children's senses and promotes developmental progress in all areas.
✦ There are several types of play and these provide the child with a variety of activities and skills.

Key tasks

1 Explain the meaning of six types of play, giving an example for each one.
2 Name four benefits of play.

Further work Observe groups of children playing together and record your findings. (IT)

Selection of toys

Children can play with a variety of household objects and get pleasure and stimulation from them because they treat them as toys. However, there is a wide range of toys on the market that are specially made to help a child learn. If toys are to be successful they should have the following factors:

+ be suitable for the age of the child
+ be strong enough
+ be suitable for the ability of the child
+ be made of safe materials
+ be made to help develop new skills
+ have some appeal to the child
+ be made to last a long time.

Safety of toys

All toys must be safe for the child to play with and should be made to meet certain safety standards. The following are safety points:

+ there should be no sharp edges
+ there should be no loose parts, e.g. eyes on dolls or teddy bears
+ painted toys should be lead-free
+ toys should have a safety mark, e.g. the CE 'lion' mark
+ toys should be strong so that they do not break easily
+ they should be free from staples and spikes.

It is also useful for toys to be washable so that they can be kept clean. This is especially important for a young baby.

Toys for different ages

Up to the age of six months, a baby is developing sensory skills such as listening, grasping, reaching out, eye movements and exploring. Suitable toys for this age would be rattles, mobiles, musical toys, soft toys and plastic keys.

At the age of six to twelve months the baby's manipulative skills are developing, as well as hand–eye co-ordination. Sensory skills are developing further, and sitting and crawling skills are also developing. Suitable toys would be push-and-pull-along toys, activity centres, building bricks and stacking beakers.

Around the age of twelve to eighteen months the child is developing balance and walking skills, can control hand movements with some accuracy and is developing language skills. Toys such as shape sorters, picture books, pop-up toys, sand and water and construction toys are ideal.

At eighteen months to two years a child is running and climbing. Hand–eye co-ordination skills are also developing further and the child is learning these skills rapidly. Suitable toys would be large jigsaws, a ball, toys with moving parts and nursery rhyme and story books.

By the age of two to three years a child is very curious and the fine manipulative skills are more developed. Gross motor skills are also improving and the child can recognize some colours and size. Suitable toys would be picture

dominoes, pencils, paints, threading beads and a tricycle.

At three to four years the child has good gross motor skills, e.g. hopping and skipping, enjoys pretend play and begins to understand mathematical concepts. Suitable toys would be a bike with stabilisers, dressing up clothes, modelling dough, a climbing frame and constructional toys.

By the age of four to five years the child has a longer concentration span and precise hand-eye co-ordination. Balance and fine manipulative skills are well developed and the imagination is developing. Suitable toys would be counting games, a clock, a pretend shop, alphabet games, weighing and measuring activities, objects useful for baking and gardening.

For further reference

For more information on suitable toys look at the Early Learning Centre catalogue or visit their website at www.elc.com

Adaptability of toys

Many toys are appropriate to children from one year right through to the age of five. They encourage a variety of different skills over the years, and provide interest for the child during

that time. An example of such a toy would be stacking beakers. These are appropriate from the age of six to twelve months, when the baby can grasp a beaker. When the child is older, he or she will learn to stack them, talk about colours, count them in number games and learn about size. The child also develops the concept of filling and emptying the beakers when playing with sand and water. The beakers also encourage social skills when playing with a group of children. When stacking the beakers, an outlet for aggression would be to knock them over, therefore expressing their emotions.

All the areas of development are covered by this simple toy across the age ranges, including social, intellectual, physical, emotional and language skills.

Key points

+ In order for toys to be successful, they should be interesting and attractive as well as strong, safe and suitable for the child.
+ The safety of a toy is of the utmost importance and several points should be looked for when buying a toy.
+ There are many toys available that cover all the areas of development and these will stimulate and encourage these skills.
+ Toys that have been bought wisely and carefully should last a long time throughout childhood.

Key tasks

1 Give seven points to look for when buying toys.
2 List five safety points to consider.
3 Suggest toys or activities for the following age groups.
  a Up to six months.
  b Between twelve and eighteen months.
  c Two to three years.
  d Four to five years.
4 Explain how a toy can last a child from babyhood to five years of age.

Further work	Design and make a toy out of household objects to develop a physical skill. Consider the safety of the toy. (RT)

Socialization

Social development is the process of children learning how to behave and how to fit in with the people around them. A child needs to develop skills and attitudes in order to be acceptable within the community in which he or she lives. Socialization means learning the social skills that enable a child to get on with others, and to behave in a way that is acceptable to others.

Parents or carers should encourage a child in the development of their social skills by:

+ providing a loving, secure home
+ encouraging opportunities for playing
+ taking the child out on visits
+ encouraging the child to share
+ setting an example on how to behave
+ giving firm, fair discipline
+ communicating with the child, e.g. at mealtimes
+ reinforcing acceptable behaviour, e.g. manners, washing hands before mealtimes.

Stages of social development

As with all areas of development, there are milestones in social development that all children pass through.

+ newborn babies cry if they are lonely and can be comforted when they are cuddled
+ at around one month, babies recognize their mother's face and will begin to smile in response to another adult
+ by three months, the baby enjoys other people's company, smiles when spoken to and enjoys feeding time
+ by six months, a baby offers toys to others, may be shy and wary of strangers and manages to feed themselves using their fingers
+ at around nine months, the baby smiles at a mirror, holds a spoon and drinks from a cup, plays alone for a while and enjoys peek-a-boo games

Playing alone

+ at twelve months old, the baby helps with feeding and dressing, enjoys hugging a familiar person and joins in conversations at mealtimes
+ at fifteen months, the child has developed self-confidence and copies others. Simple household tasks are enjoyed, e.g. dusting
+ by the age of eighteen months, the child continues to play alone, is keen to dress themselves, can hold a cup and feed themselves quite well. The child is slowly becoming more independent in some skills

Showing independence

+ at two years of age, the child may be independent sometimes but at other times may be dependent and cling to a familiar person. They will eat independently and call themselves by their own name
+ at around two and a half years of age, the child is involved in **parallel play**, goes to the toilet independently (but may need some help with their clothing) and is competent with a spoon and perhaps a fork
+ by the age of three years, the child may be dry at night, can do some dressing and undressing, enjoys pretend play and family mealtimes, helps adults to tidy up, takes part in **joining in play** and makes friends
+ at around the age of four years, the child becomes involved in **co-operative play**, can wash and dry hands, cleans teeth, undresses and dresses (except for laces and fastenings at the back)

Dressing unaided

✦ by five years of age, the child chooses his or her own friends, comforts others if they are upset, eats correctly, enjoys caring for animals, and knows his or her full name and address. A child of this age can keep themselves occupied for a long time by looking at a book or video.

Children are not born with these social skills – they have to learn them. It is therefore the parent's or carer's responsibility to teach them if the child is to behave in an acceptable way.

The influence of the environment

A child's environment can influence the way their social skills develop. If the child lives in a remote country area, it may be difficult to have contact with others of the same age, or if the child comes from a well-off family, they may have everything they want and may not want to share their possessions. A child from a poor family may be jealous of others who have more toys than them. The size of the family can also influence the child's social development. A child living in a large family will learn the social skill of sharing with others, but may experience the disadvantages of not having so much adult attention. An only child will have the advantage of adult attention, but will not have the opportunities within the family of sharing and playing.

Whatever environment a child is growing up in, it is the responsibility of the parents or carers to provide the child with as many different opportunities as possible in order for the child to develop a wide range of social skills. It is important that a child is brought up in a secure and loving background in order to develop positive social skills and become acceptable in their behaviour towards others. Parents or carers should show the child that he or she are loved constantly, regardless of the child's behaviour, and provide a stable, secure home where the child feels safe, and knows that he or she has someone for support and encouragement.

Key points

✦ Social development is about learning how to behave in an acceptable way.
✦ Children have to learn social skills from the people around them – they are not born with this knowledge.
✦ Parents or carers should encourage and stimulate a child's social skills.
✦ The environment, financial position and size of the family all have an influence on the way the child develops their social skills.

Key tasks

1 Suggest six ways a parent or carer can encourage a child in developing their social skills.
2 Give an average age for the following stages of social development:
   a May be wary of strangers.
   b Enjoys hugging a familiar person.
   c Copies others.
   d Becomes more independent.
   e Can dress and undress apart from any shoelaces.
3 Explain how the following can influence a child's social skills.
   a The environment.
   b The family's financial position.
   c The size of the family.

Further work · Observe a group of children in a playgroup situation. Take notes on any social skills or lack of them that you may notice. (IT)

Social play

Learning to play with other children is an important part of social development. There are several stages of social play, and as a child goes through each one it learns how to communicate and get on with other children.

Stages of play

Solitary play

Solitary play means playing alone. Babies and young children spend a long time quite happily playing on their own with toys, or carrying out activities.

Parallel play

In parallel play, the child is gaining in confidence and is happy to play beside another child. The children may be doing the same activity, but will not play together yet.

Looking-on play

Looking-on play involves a child watching other children play. The child still plays alone, but is a spectator of play and watches from the edge of a group without playing.

Joining-in play

In this type of play, a child joins in with another child or group of children and does the same activity as all the children but in his or her own way.

Co-operative play

Co-operative play is when children play together, either with another child or in a group. In this play, the children are sharing activities and communicating with each other, e.g. playing a game of football or making biscuits.

Link: *For more information on the stages of development see pages 38–43.*

Social behaviour

Parents or carers must encourage children to behave in an acceptable manner in order for them to get on with others. Children should be praised whenever they have shown correct social behaviour, e.g. saying 'please' and 'thank you', taking turns and helping others. If children are encouraged and praised whenever they behave in a socially acceptable way, they will be eager to do it again.

Negative behaviour

Children are naturally not going to behave well all the time. They are often naughty, and this can be shown in the following ways:

+ temper tantrums
+ lying
+ aggression towards others
+ attention-seeking behaviour.

Temper tantrums

Temper tantrums usually occur between the ages of two and three years, and are brought on because the child becomes frustrated. The child should be left until he or she has calmed down. The child can then be reasoned with and needs to be shown that this behaviour is not acceptable.

Lying

Lying is a common form of unacceptable behaviour. A child does not know the difference between pretend play and real life at times, and this is where the confusion can occur. The parent or carer needs to understand this and help the child be aware of truths and lies.

Aggression towards others

Aggression towards others can be in the form of kicking, biting, shouting, and so on. A parent or carer needs to be patient, and careful handling of the situation should ensure that the child settles into a more acceptable way of behaving.

Attention-seeking behaviour

Attention-seeking is very common in children between the ages of one and four years. Children like to be the centre of attention. If they achieve this by behaving in a certain way, which goes unchecked by their parents or carers, then it will become a habit. Examples include:

+ refusing to eat
+ holding their breath
+ refusing to use the toilet
+ screaming.

If the parent or carer ignores this behaviour, children will learn that they are not getting the attention that they want and will stop.

A child's personality will play a part in how he or she behaves – e.g. a child who is shy will need to be encouraged to be friendly towards others. Children should be encouraged to bring out the positive side of their personalities and to control the negative side.

Key points

+ There are several stages of social play that a child goes through in order to learn how to socialize with others.
+ Children need to know that they must learn to behave in a socially acceptable way.

Key tasks

1 Describe five types of social play.
2 Suggest four ways a child may show acceptable social behaviour.
3 Describe ways in which a parent or carer should handle situations of unacceptable behaviour.

Further work

Observe a child's behaviour when playing in a group of children. Write down any social or anti-social behaviour that may be demonstrated. (IT)

Discipline

Children need to learn how to behave, and this will affect their social and emotional development. A child needs to know how to control his or her feelings (emotional) and how to behave in an acceptable manner (social). Parents or carers play an important role in teaching a child how to behave. Discipline is needed so that a child will learn.

Discipline is often a difficult job, but parents or carers need to consider the following points:

+ set a good example
+ be consistent
+ praise the child for good behaviour
+ avoid confrontation with the child
+ if the child is behaving in an unacceptable way, divert the child's attention to another activity
+ apologize if they (the parents/carers) have behaved badly, e.g. by being short-tempered.

Discipline needs to be fair, firm, consistent and understood by the child. Children will benefit from discipline in the following ways:

+ it helps them learn self-control
+ it helps them behave in an acceptable way
+ it makes them feel secure and safe.

Levels of discipline

Too much or not enough discipline are both harmful to a child, and will not help the child learn how to behave. Too much discipline may:

+ cause the child to be miserable
+ put too many expectations on the child
+ harm the relationship between the child and parent/carer as it means the parent/carer is constantly telling the child off.

The child who has too much discipline may be expected to be good all the time and is constantly being told 'don't do that, do this'. H or she may feel that they cannot do anything right, and this may result in them doing nothin because they are frightened of being told off if they do.

On the other hand, not enough discipline may:

+ cause the child to feel insecure
+ encourage the child to be rude and selfish
+ encourage disobedience in the child.

An undisciplined child will become spoilt, unruly and will have no thought for others. He or she will expect everything they want, and may feel insecure as there are no boundaries on behaviour. The child will also be at risk from accidents as they will be unaware of dangers.

At what age can discipline begin?

Discipline can only begin when a child can understand what is expected of him or her. By the age of one year, a child will understand the word 'no' and so will begin to be aware of what he or she can and cannot do. After this age, as the child grows older with greater understanding, he or she will gradually become aware of what is expected.

Praise or punishment?

Discipline involves both praise and punishment. A child who has behaved well must be rewarded so that he or she understands what is expected and to encourage further good behaviour. Verbal praise is the most effective way of rewarding a child, but, for something special, a parent or carer may offer a present as a means of praise.

If a child has behaved badly, he or she needs to be aware that this is not acceptable. Punishment cannot be given unless the child understands, so a child under one year of age should not be punished as this will cause confusion. However, if a baby of this age is doing something that is not acceptable, e.g. emptying the soil from a house plant, the parent or carer should either remove the plant, or distract the child with an acceptable activity such as drawing.

Distracting the child with a suitable activity

Punishment

Here are some ways a parent or carer may punish a child over the age of one year:

◆ by showing they are not pleased with the child's behaviour, e.g. by ignoring the child for a while or by putting the child to sit in the corner

◆ by explaining, for example, why the hot cup should not be touched – if the child can be reasoned with

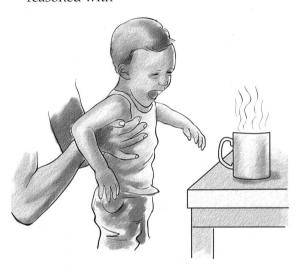

Children aged about two can be reasoned with

◆ by withdrawing the activity or item that caused the problem, e.g. if the child has been scribbling on a wall or chair, remove the pens or crayons for a set time.

Scribbling on a wall is unacceptable behaviour

Whatever punishment is dealt out to a child, it should be effective and should happen straight away. A parent or carer should never say, 'Wait until daddy or mummy comes home' – by the time this happens the child will have forgotten what they are being punished for. Parents or carers should never make a threat of punishment unless they intend to carry it out. If a child is told, 'Eat your dinner or you won't get any sweets', and then has the sweets anyway, he or she will never learn to be obedient.

It is not necessary to smack a child in order to teach a child how to behave. A child who is regularly smacked may, in turn, smack or hit others.

Key points

◆ Discipline is required in order for a child to learn how to behave and how to control his or her feelings.

◆ Parents or carers should ensure that discipline is fair, firm and that the child understands what is expected of him or her.

◆ A child will suffer if there is too much or not enough discipline.

◆ Children should be given praise for good behaviour and some form of punishment for bad behaviour.

◆ Punishment should be carried out immediately, but smacking is not necessary as a method of punishment.

Key tasks

1 Why do children need to be disciplined?
2 Suggest six ways a parent or carer can help discipline a child.
3 What are the effects of the following?
  a Too much discipline.
  b Not enough discipline.
4 Name three ways a parent could discipline a child over the age of one year.

Stages of emotional development

Emotional development is the development of a child's emotions. Children need to learn how to control their emotions in order to be acceptable within the community that they live. Emotional development is linked with other areas, but particularly with social development.

> Link: *For more information on social development see pages 86–89.*

Emotions and socialization are closely linked, as children need to feel secure and loved in order to develop their own personality in a way that is acceptable in society.

Positive and negative emotions

Everyone experiences both positive and negative emotions and these feelings can often get mixed up. Positive emotions, e.g. happiness, joy, pleasure, love and excitement, need to be encouraged. Negative emotions, e.g. anger, guilt, hate, jealousy and impatience should be controlled. All these emotions are going to be felt at some time and the child needs to learn how to control these feelings.

Parents or carers should be aware that children should be allowed to express these emotions through play (e.g. role-play) so that they can experience positive and negative feelings. Parents or carers should provide opportunities for their child to play in this way, as it will encourage him or her to develop personality and independence.

The child's personality

The child's personality develops gradually over a long period of time – up to five years. Babies and young children under the age of two years think that they are the most important person, and that everything and everybody revolves around them. After the age of two years, children begin to respond to those around them. They start to care for younger children and show some understanding towards the needs of others.

How a child develops emotionally depends on its character, the genes he or she has inherited and the way he or she feels about themselves. The influence of friends, family and the environment will shape a child's personality.

Stages of emotional development

As with other areas of development, a child passes through different stages. These milestones that are reached are the average age only, and each child develops at a different pace.

+ newborn babies use body movements to express pleasure, e.g. when being fed
+ at one month, the baby begins to show some personality, e.g. calm or excitable
+ by three months, the baby enjoys company and routines, e.g. bathtime

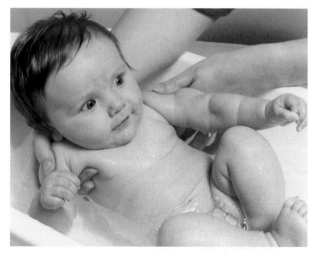

Enjoying bathtime

+ at around six months, the baby may develop shyness and becomes upset when their mother leaves the room
+ at nine months, the baby expresses negative emotions, e.g. anger, may use a comfort toy, develops a fear of strangers and develops likes and dislikes, e.g. food at mealtimes
+ by twelve months, the baby seeks attention and reassurance from adults and shows affection to familiar people
+ by fifteen months, the child begins to co-operate with others but may also begin to have temper tantrums. The child's moods may swing from a positive to a negative emotion fairly rapidly

A temper tantrum

- at eighteen months, the child develops more independence, expresses rage and frustration and shows strong emotions
- at around two years, temper tantrums may be more frequent and the child may become more curious about their environment
- at two and a half years, the child may have fears about the surroundings or people they are familiar with for no reason, e.g. fear of the dark
- by the age of three years, the child begins to care for a younger child, independence is developing further and the child becomes more stable and emotionally secure

Caring for a younger child

- by four years old, the child may develop a sense of humour, expresses many emotions through 'pretend' or imaginative play and will be strongly self-willed
- at the age of five years, the child shows sympathy to others who are hurt, has very definite likes and dislikes and may be happy to leave parents or carers for a while, e.g. to go to school.

Key points

- ✦ Emotional development is linked to all areas of development but especially socialization.
- ✦ There are many feelings that a child experiences, and parents or carers should provide opportunities in play for the child to be able to express these feelings.
- ✦ There are several stages of emotional development that a child passes through.
- ✦ A child's personality will depend on the genes inherited and the influence of everyone around him or her.

Key tasks

1 What do you understand by the term 'emotional development'?
2 List four positive and four negative emotions.
3 Suggest two factors that influence a child's personality.
4 Give the average age for the following emotional development milestones:

   a Becomes upset when their mother leaves.

   b Shows affection to familiar people.

   c Has frequent temper tantrums.

   d Develops a sense of humour.

Further work	Observe and record any emotions a child may demonstrate during activities that may be taking place, e.g. at mealtimes, bathtimes or an organized play session. (IT)

Conditions for emotional development

Bonding

Bonds of affection between mother and baby

The bonding of a baby and the parents or carers in the first days of the baby's life is very important. Bonding means the feelings of love and affection between the parents or carers and the baby.

These feelings develop during the early days after the birth, providing the baby is cuddled closely, and this helps babies develop feelings and emotions towards the people around them. The love given freely by parents or carers is often called **unconditional love**, meaning that they give that love without any conditions such as whether the child is well behaved or not.

Immediately after birth, the mother is given the baby to cuddle and hold close. Skin and eye contact play an important part in developing strong bonds of affection. Holding the baby close, e.g. at feeding time, will encourage these bonds to develop and help make the baby feel secure and comforted. It is important that the father also develops these bonds of affection and, if he is present at the birth, he will be involved straight away.

Environmental factors

The environment that children grow up in plays an important part in the way they develop emotionally. This includes the home conditions, the way in which the child is brought up and life experiences.

The following are conditions necessary for the development of the emotions in a child:

- to have love and affection from parents or carers and friends around the baby
- to be given opportunities to be independent
- to be valued as individuals
- to have encouraged acceptable behaviour
- to be reassured and helped to develop confidence
- to feel secure in relationships with others.

If these conditions are met by the parents or carers, the child will feel safe and secure. A child will progress in a positive way if he or she has this security. At times, however, children may feel insecure and may develop fears about something that is happening in their life. The insecure child may feel unwanted and behave badly in order to get attention from parents or carers. They may develop negative emotions such as jealousy, shyness, rudeness and aggression. Usually, a child will overcome many of these insecurities if given plenty of love and attention from parents or carers.

Regression

Some children may regress in their behaviour. Regression means that the child can go backwards in an area of development that he or she has already acquired, e.g. if a child has been dry at night he or she may start to wet the bed again.

The source of the insecurity needs to be identified so that the problem can be dealt with. For example, if the child is feeling worried about starting school and this has caused the regression, providing the parent or carer deals with this in a calm and patient manner and talks to the child, the problem can be sorted out and the child will, given time, stop wetting the bed again. If the child is constantly shouted at about wetting the bed and is not spoken to or helped with the problem, no improvement will be made.

Sibling rivalry

The term 'sibling' means a brother or a sister. **Sibling rivalry** means that the child may feel a brother or sister is getting more attention than him or herself. This can be very common when a new baby is born in the family. Obviously, the baby will be getting a lot of attention and the sibling may feel left out. The sibling may have feelings of jealousy towards the new baby and he or she may express these feelings by:

+ becoming clingy towards the parents or carers
+ hitting out at someone
+ pinching
+ taking toys away from others
+ becoming withdrawn
+ regressing in behaviour.

Parents or carers need to be aware of these feelings and should:

+ involve the child with the coming birth of the baby
+ encourage him or her to help choose items for the baby
+ offer plenty of affection
+ talk to the child about the baby
+ say how important the child is within the family
+ encourage the child to help with the baby when it arrives.

All these ways will help the child to feel secure and overcome their feelings of jealousy.

Fears and nightmares

Children may develop fears that are very real to them, e.g. the dark, animals, insects and noises. A child's imagination starts to develop at around the age of two years and it is this development, linked with lack of understanding, that causes these fears. Nightmares may be a result of these fears, and a child who has nightmares regularly must be comforted and reassured. Sometimes they are linked with a major life event such as starting school or unhappiness in the home. Nightmares usually stop once the cause has been dealt with.

Comforters

Many children have a comforter such as a soft toy, a piece of cloth or a blanket. These offer security to the child, especially at night, and the child becomes very attached to the comforter. Children will grow out of these comforters, but may need them for several years.

Comforters are important for some children

Key points

+ It is important that bonding is developed in the first days of a baby's life in order to establish feelings of love and affection between the parents or carers and the baby.
+ Parents or carers should meet several conditions of emotional development in order for the child to feel safe and secure.
+ A child who feels insecure may have negative feelings and these may be shown in a variety of ways.

Key tasks

1 What is meant by the term 'bonding'?
2 Suggest six conditions of emotional development.
3 How may an insecure child show his or her feelings?
4 a Explain the following terms:
  i Regression
  ii Sibling rivalry.
  b How should a parent or carer react to each situation?

Family structures

What is a family?

A family is a group of people who live together or who are related by marriage or blood. This includes those couples who **co-habit**, which means that they live together without being married. The family forms the basic unit of society in the United Kingdom today. It provides for the basic needs of the individuals in the family group. The traditional image of the family unit of two adults and two children is only one of many different types of family structures.

As the United Kingdom becomes a wider multicultural society, there is more variety in the type and structure of family units. For example, many families with ethnic origins in Asia have extended family structures that often have three generations living together. These families place great value on the role of the older generation in the structure and functions of family life. Society is more multicultural today, with individuals from differing ethnic and cultural backgrounds marrying and forming new family units.

A nuclear family

Types of families

The nuclear family

The nuclear family consists of parents and dependent children living together. It is the most common type of family unit. The parents often bring up the children without

The nuclear family

help from other relations such as grandparents, as they may live a long way from the family. Sometimes parents work outside the home and children are cared for by people who are not related.

The extended family

The **extended family** is a nuclear family extended by grandparents or other relations such as aunts or uncles. The extended family was traditionally a more common family type in the United Kingdom, but social changes such as the changing pattern of work opportunities has meant a generation of a family often moves away for work. The extended family has many advantages, such as having more adults in the household to care for the children. In many cultures the extended family is the most common form of family structure, with perhaps three generations of a family living together.

The extended family

The lone-parent family

There are an increasing number of **lone-parent families** in the United Kingdom. Approximately 25 per cent of all families with dependent children are lone-parent families. The lone-parent family has one parent, usually the mother, looking after the child or children. Some lone-parent families were originally nuclear or extended families but the family structure has changed. The lone-parent may be unmarried, separated or divorced.

The lone-parent family

The reconstituted family

Reconstituted families are families that have changed in structure and reformed in a new way. They are also called **modified** or **step families**.

These families usually have at least one child who is the natural child of one parent but not both. The family may be made up of children from both parents' previous relationships. In 2000, about one in twelve children were part of a reconstituted family.

The reconstituted family

The functions of the family

The functions of the family are to provide for the needs of the family members. These needs will vary depending on the individuals who make up the family and the cultural background. The primary functions of the family are to provide for:

✦ the basic physical needs of shelter, food, warmth and clothing
✦ protection and support
✦ love and security
✦ opportunities for learning and development.

Socialization in the family

Socialization is another key function of the family. Children need to learn how to live in society, and how to behave and act in different situations – this is called socialization. The family plays an important role in the socialization of the child. The way people think and behave is related to the way they have been brought up. The family gives the child his or her sense of values. Adults are influenced in their approach to parenthood by their own upbringing. Today's children will be the future citizens who will, as parents, go on to raise children of their own.

Social structures elsewhere

In other parts of the world, different social and family structures occur. One well-known structure is that of the **kibbutz** communities. In Israel about five per cent of the population live in large communities called kibbutzim, which are collective farms. Adults share the work on the farms and the children of the kibbutzim grow up in a separate area and are cared for by others. They have regular contact with their parents so there is still some evidence of family structure in the community. The advantage of this system is that the children brought up in the kibbutz feel a greater responsibility towards the needs of the community as a whole.

An extended family is a different type of family structure

Key points

✦ The family forms the basic unit of society.
✦ The four main types of family structure in the United Kingdom are nuclear, extended, lone-parent and reconstituted.
✦ The family plays a key role in the socialization of children.
✦ There are different family structures in other cultures.

Key tasks

1 Describe the four main types of family structures in the United Kingdom.
2 Explain how the family helps the socialization of children.
3 What is the advantage of the kibbutzim system?

Further work | Find out and write a short report about two other different types of family structures or family patterns in other cultures. (IT/RT)

Changing patterns of family life

Families are in a constant state of change as individuals in the family grow older and become more or less dependent on others. The pattern of family life changes. Social changes in society, such as attitudes to marriage, will affect the pattern of family life. The changes happen to the structure of the family and to the roles and relationships within the family. Reasons for the changes to the structure of the family include the following:

✦ changes in the divorce law has made divorce easier for couples. There has been an increase in the number of divorces which, in turn, changes the type of family structures that children are raised in

✦ changes in the expectation of lifestyles of men and women affects the age at which people choose to marry, have children and how they split and divide the family responsibilities

✦ the availability of methods of contraception allow families to plan when to have children. Families are now smaller than they were 50 years ago

✦ changing social and moral attitudes to marriage, which means many couples co-habit and sometimes relationships are less stable. This can lead to an increase in the number of lone-parent families

✦ changes in social welfare system, which offers support to families and can often enable lone-parent families to live independently.

Link: *For more information on lone-parent families see pages 106–107.*

Changing roles within the family

The roles in the family are changing. Traditionally the father went out to work to provide financially for the family, and the mother stayed at home to look after the children. Changes in society today have meant this happens in fewer family structures. Although the mother still often takes on more of the child-caring responsibilities in the home, the balance of the care is changing. For example:

✦ when couples marry these days they may have different attitudes and expectations in marriage to those of their parents, and they regard family life as a joint sharing and caring role

✦ employment patterns have changed – with more women working by necessity or choice, this changes the roles within the family

✦ the role of women in society is changing. As more women take active roles outside the home, it affects their status in the home.

Couples share family responsibilities

Shared roles

Most couples starting to have families today see family responsibilities as a shared role. The mother and father do not have separate roles. They may both work and contribute towards the family finances and share the caring and household tasks. The advantages of families where both parents share the roles are:

✦ with both parents or carers working the family's standard of living will probably improve
✦ fathers have the opportunity to have a closer relationship with their children than in the tradition family role
✦ children will benefit from a range of caring styles
✦ children are brought up with the attitude that families share responsibilities, which will, in turn, influence their view of family life when they grow up.

The increase in lone-parent families

One of the major changes in family structures is the increase in the number of lone-parent families. The rise in the divorce rate is one reason for this increase. The increase in the number of pregnancies outside marriage is another. The changes in social attitudes make it more acceptable today for a child to be brought up in a lone-parent family. Lone parents, like all families with dependent children, come from all ethnic groups.

Lone mothers are the largest group of lone parents

Spring 2000						
Great Britain						Percentages
	White	Black	Indian	Pakistani/ Bangladeshi	Other groups[2]	All ethnic groups[3]
Couples	79	51	92	85	71	78
Lone parents	21	49	8	15	29	22
All[4] (=100%) (millions)	6.6	0.2	0.2	0.2	0.3	7.2

Source: Labour Force Survey, Office for National Statistics

Families with dependent children

The lone parent has to take on the responsibility of two parents. Many lone parents provide happy, stable and caring homes for their children, but some lone parents need additional help and financial support.

Link: *For more information on financial support see pages 104–105.*

Key points

✦ Social changes have affected family structures.
✦ Most couples getting married today see family responsibilities as a shared role.
✦ The role of women in society is changing and affecting their status in the home.
✦ There is an increase in the number of lone-parent families.

Key tasks

1 Explain the reasons for the changes in the structure of the family.
2 How have roles within the family changed over the last 25 years?
3 Outline the reasons why lone-parent families are often more dependent on support than other types of family structures.

Further work Use the internet to find statistics about changing family structures. (RT/IT)

Looked-after children

The social services take responsibility for children taken into the care of the local authority. These children are referred to as **looked-after children**. All agencies that care for children agree that the best place for children is with their families, but there are situations where this is not possible. This may be because:

+ the parent or parents are unable to look after the child because they are ill or in hospital
+ there is evidence of neglect of the child
+ there is evidence of abuse of the child.

If the social services department feel the child is at risk, they obtain a care order from the court to take the child in to **compulsory care**. Families can ask for their children to be taken into care if they feel they are unable to cope with them.

Residential care for children

Residential homes try to provide a family type of structure for children in their care. Adult carers take responsibility for small groups of children to build up a secure and caring relationship with them. Children who are taken in to compulsory care have often not experienced the continuity of family life. It is sometimes decided that residential care is the best course of action for some children.

Some children are placed in residential care homes

Here are some reasons why children are placed in residential homes:

+ special support and treatment are required, which can best be met by the trained staff in the community unit
+ children in the same family can be kept together

+ the child may have poor experience of **foster care**
+ abuse has occurred within the family, which makes living with another family unsuitable.

Residential care homes provide short-term care for children. It is recognized that they are not the ideal place for them to prepare to live their adult lives in society. Although they play a valuable part in the care system, wherever possible children are placed in foster care.

Foster care

When a child is fostered he or she is placed with another family that will care for and support the child and treat him or her as part of the family. Foster carers need to enjoy looking after children, as many of the children they foster may be emotionally upset and vulnerable. Foster carers do not have any legal rights over a child. They are paid an allowance to cover their expenses in caring for the child.

The length of time a child is in foster care will vary with the individual circumstances of the child. Foster care can be on a long or short-term basis:

+ long-term fostering – the child settles into a pattern of living with the foster family as part of their family
+ short-term fostering – to meet a short-term need the child is placed temporarily with foster carers, for example when the social services have intervened and removed a child from a situation.

The role of foster care

There are more children placed in foster care than in residential care homes as it is thought to be a better type of care for looked-after children. This is because:

+ it gives the child a family structure and the opportunity to develop relationships with family members
+ it allows the child the chance to develop as an individual
+ the foster carers can be more flexible to meet the needs of the individual child than care workers in a residential unit, who have a larger number of children to look after.

Regulation of foster care

Foster carers are checked by the social services department to make sure they are suitable to accept responsibility for children in their care. They follow guidelines laid down in the Children Act (1989), which include:

+ allowing access to the child's natural parents when it is thought to be in the child's interest
+ bringing up the child in the child's own religion
+ looking after the child with the same care as they would look after their own child
+ returning the child to local authority care when asked.

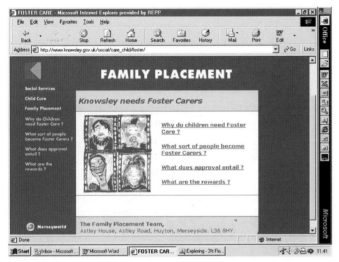

Local authorities advertize for foster carers

Adoption

Adoption is the legal process where adults become parents to children they have not given birth to. The adoptive parents will have full legal rights over the child. The adoption process is long and complex. Couples wishing to adopt approach adoption agencies, which can be the local authority or another independent agency such as National Children's Home.

Traditionally couples adopted newly born or very young babies, but social changes in society have reduced the number of babies available for adoption. These changes include:

+ increasing availability of birth control
+ improved support structure for lone mothers to keep babies born outside marriage
+ society's acceptance of babies born outside marriage.

The number of children available for adoption has reduced from 21 000 in 1975 to just over 4000 in 2000. Children available for adoption are often older or children with special needs.

The differences between foster care and adoption

Both fostering and adoption are alternative ways of forming or extending families, but the responsibility the adults have for the child in their care is different (see table below).

Responsibilities of fostering and adoption

A foster parent has:	An adoptive parent has:
+ no legal rights over the child	+ legal rights over the child
+ an allowance to cover the cost of bringing up the child	+ to financially cover the cost of bringing up the child
+ temporary responsibility for the child.	+ permanent responsibility for the child.

Key points

+ Children are taken into local authority care when their parents are unable to look after them, or when there is evidence of neglect or abuse.
+ Foster care is seen to be a suitable type of care for children, as it provides a secure family environment.
+ There is a reduction in the number of children available for adoption.

Key tasks

1 Explain why children may be taken into the care of the local authority.
2 Suggest reasons why foster care is thought to be the best option for looked-after children.
3 Describe the differences between adoption and fostering.

Day-care provision

The need for day-care provision

There is an increase in the need for day-care provision because:

✦ many families have one or both parents or carers working, and need to find other carers for their children during the day
✦ it is recognized that children benefit from early years experiences before they start formal school
✦ the child may have special needs and require special provision to enable them to make progress.

Increase in the use of childcare places

	1975	2000
Nurseries	53 000	247 000
Childminders	83 500	337 700

Many working parents or carers use some formal childcare arrangements, whilst other parents or carers use informal support such as family and friends.

The Children Act (1989) requires local authorities to provide a range of day-care services for children under five. A quarter of all three- and four-year-olds receive some type of pre-school or nursery education.

There is a wide range of day-care provision available to children under five years of age:

✦ day nurseries
✦ nursery schools
✦ childminders
✦ playgroups.

Day nurseries

Day nurseries offer a range of care where children are looked after during their parents' or carers' working hours. Some are run by the local authorities, others by the employer or educational institute and some are run privately. All day nurseries need to be registered and must follow government guidelines about staffing, facilities, safety and other practical issues. The social services department uses these guidelines from the Children Act to assess the quality of provision at the day nursery. Day nurseries are widely used because they:

✦ provide children with good, basic care to standards which are clearly laid down
✦ operate hours to suit the needs of working parents
✦ give children opportunities for socialization with other children in a structured environment
✦ provide a wide range of resources, activities and learning opportunities.

Workplace crèches

Workplace crèches or nurseries are a form of day nursery provision provided to meet the needs of the workforce. They are often on the employer's premises and run to the same standards as other nurseries.

A workplace crèche is a convenient form of day care

Nursery schools

Nursery schools are different from day nurseries as they provide a more formal educational setting. Government policy has been to increase the number of children attending nursery schools. Most local authorities offer some nursery school provision for children under the age of five. Nursery school provision is also available privately. Nursery schools are subject to regulation and inspection to make sure the guidelines that are laid down for them are followed.

Childminders

Childminders provide a care service for young children in a home environment, looking after only a few children at a time. Most childminders look after up to three young children, including any of their own. They are required by the Children Act (1989) to be registered by the local authority and to meet certain standards. A list of registered childminders is available from the local social services department, who will visit the childminder on a regular basis to inspect the quality of care on offer.

Reasons parents or carers may choose a childminder include:

+ hours can often be more flexible to suit the needs of working parents
+ the home environment may be seen as more appropriate and less threatening for the very young child
+ it is sometimes a cheaper form of childcare provision
+ the child may be with other young children in a family environment.

Playgroups

Playgroups are usually held in local premises such as village halls for morning sessions only. They are for children aged between three and five years old, who usually attend for two or three mornings a week. Playgroups are managed by qualified staff who are specially trained to work with children of this age. Playgroups are often referred to as pre-schools. Until recently they were the most popular form of pre-school provision but the numbers of children attending playgroup have reduced. This may be because:

+ more women are working and need full-time day-care provision for their children, which the playgroup cannot provide
+ there is an increasing provision for pre-school education in nursery school places in the local primary school.

Playgroups are recognized as part of the pre-school education provision for the under fives. The child has the opportunity to learn through play in a wide range of activities from water play to imaginative play. Playgroups are now inspected to assess the value of the education provision. Most playgroups belong to the Pre-school Learning Alliance.

Flexible work practices

Many employers have developed new initiatives to meet the needs of working parents. These new practices give parents and carers more

A range of activities are provided in playgroups

flexibility in their childcare arrangements. For example:

+ job sharing – a practice where two people share one job and one salary to enable them to have the benefits of continuing employment, but to have time with their children while they are growing up
+ flexible hours – this is a more common practice today to enable parents and carers to fit their working day around their childcare arrangements, e.g. they start earlier and finish earlier
+ working from home – with modern communication systems this is becoming a popular option for some parents and carers.

Key tasks

1 Explain why there is an increase in the need for day-care provision.
2 Why do many parents and carers choose to use a childminder to look after their young child?

Further work	Carry out a survey in your local area to find out what day-care provision is available. Present your results as a report. (RT/IT)

The community

A community is a group of people living in a local area. The needs of communities in the United Kingdom are met by local authorities and other government agencies such as the National Health Service. These agencies have a statutory duty, which means they are directed by law to look after the needs of individuals and families in the community. Services provided to meet the needs of the community include:

✦ meeting the personal needs of the family for housing, education and health
✦ providing community facilities in the local area such as parks, sports centres and libraries
✦ protecting the family by the provision of emergency services (fire, ambulance and police)
✦ supplying environmental services to include street cleaning, refuse and recycling.

Community Provision

Statutory support for families

Statutory support is provided for families as part of the **social security system** in the United Kingdom. Many families need help and support to provide for their members. The support offered will depend on the particular needs of the family, but it can be practical (such as help in finding appropriate housing), financial (such as receiving benefits) or advisory (such as help in managing a special needs child).

Financial support for families

A range of benefits and tax credits are available to families who can get advice and information from their local benefits agency office.

Means testing

For families to receive some types of financial support they are **means tested**. This is when the income of the family is compared with a standard amount of money to assess if they are in need of financial support. Means-tested benefits are said to be targeted, which means they are directed at the families most in need. Means-tested benefits include:

✦ **Working Families' Tax Credit** to support families on low income but who are in employment and have at least one child
✦ **income support** is a benefit for those people whose income falls below a given level of money, and who are not working or are working less than sixteen hours a week
✦ **housing benefit** and **council tax benefit** to assist in the costs of housing for families on low incomes
✦ **sure start maternity grants**, which help pay for the costs of a new baby. It is a single payment for families on low income.

Working Families' Tax Credit

Working Families' Tax Credit replaces Family Credit. The amount received varies depending on the family income, number of children, and so on. The benefit is paid as a tax credit in the pay packet of the parent in employment. It is available to couples and lone parents who:

✦ have one or more children
✦ work at least sixteen hours a week
✦ have savings of £8000 or less.

Passport benefits

Working Families' Tax Credit and income support are often referred to as **passport benefits**, which means that if people receive these benefits, they also receive other benefits such as free medical treatment for all family members.

Information provided by the benefits agency

Universal benefits

Universal benefits are benefits available to everyone entitled to receive the benefit regardless of income, such as child benefit. These benefits are targeted at specific groups such as children or the disabled. Universal benefits include:

✦ **child benefit** is an allowance paid to a parent of every child. The allowance is paid until the child leaves full-time education or is 18 years of age. Nearly all parents accept child benefit for their child

✦ **disability allowance** is paid to help cover the costs of caring for a disabled child or adult

✦ free dental treatment and medical prescriptions are an entitlement for all children until they leave full-time education.

Key tasks

1 Explain the difference between means-tested and universal benefits.

2 Describe the services that are provided for families in the community.

Key points

✦ The community provides a wide range of services for families.

✦ Information about financial support for families is available at the local benefits agency office.

✦ Means-tested benefits are targeted at families in greatest need.

✦ Universal benefits are available to everyone, regardless of income.

Further work

1 Use a map of your local area to identify where services provided to the community are located. (RT/IT)

2 Collect a selection of current benefits agency leaflets from your local post office or benefits agency office. Prepare a short presentation to explain one of the benefits available to a family. (RT/IT)

Social services

Personal social services

The personal social services are designed to meet the social needs of vulnerable groups in society such as children and families in need of support. The services are provided by the local authority or voluntary and private organizations. Social workers play a key role in the provision of the personal social services. Access to these services is by referral, which means the social services are initially contacted by the local GP, health visitor or a parent or carer themselves. Social workers deal with many family issues such as:

+ parenting problems
+ financial problems for a family
+ violence in the home
+ child protection
+ provision of statutory services.

Social workers who operate in the local authority are often referred to as **field social workers**. They have a multi-disciplinary approach, which means they work with government and voluntary organizations to support and help individuals and families to live a normal life in the community. Their work will often include visiting families in their own homes. They refer to the individuals or families they deal with as clients. Activities of a field social worker include:

+ signposting – directing the client to specialist help such as a debt counsellor or benefits agency office
+ advocacy – meaning that the social worker acts on the behalf of the family (client) to help put across the client's point of view. This could, for example, be in the case of a legal matter that has come to court
+ assessment – where social workers are able to identify the needs of individuals or families in order to offer the appropriate support and guidance.

The needs of the lone-parent family

Many lone-parent families are dependent on support from social services departments in the local authority. Field social workers play a key role in assessing the needs of lone-parent families and directing them to suitable resources

Social workers offer support to families

and advice agencies. Lone-parent families are more likely to have low incomes and to be dependent on social welfare for financial support. This is because lone parents:

+ may have become parents before they had the financial means to provide for the basic needs of their family
+ are mostly women who are more likely to have low paid, possibly part-time, work
+ have to care for the children on their own so they may not be able to work.

Child Support Agency

The **Child Support Agency** was established in 1993 to help support lone-parent families. Any lone parent who receives Income Support or Working Families' Tax Credit is required by law to give details of the absent parent, who will be asked to contribute towards the costs of caring for the child. The Child Support Agency has a responsibility to make sure the absent parent contributes towards the maintenance of his or her child.

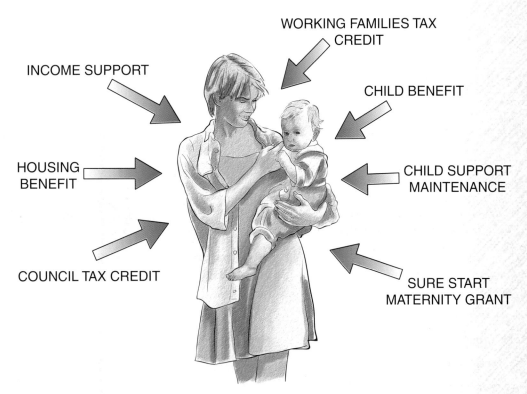

INCOME SUPPORT

WORKING FAMILIES TAX CREDIT

CHILD BENEFIT

HOUSING BENEFIT

CHILD SUPPORT MAINTENANCE

COUNCIL TAX CREDIT

SURE START MATERNITY GRANT

Benefits that may be available for the lone parent

Take-up of benefits

Many families who are entitled to benefits do not apply for them. This may be because:

+ they may not know what benefits they are entitled to
+ the forms may be too difficult and complex for them to complete
+ there may be a language barrier, which prevents the family applying for the benefits
+ they may be embarrassed about applying for them.

Welfare to Work Scheme

The Welfare to Work Scheme is a government initiative to encourage people on benefits to find jobs and so become less dependent on welfare provision.

Lone parents were one of the groups that are targeted for this programme. The scheme helps with advice, training and reskilling to open up job opportunities. An important part of the scheme is to give support and financial assistance with childcare. A network of after-school clubs was also set up to provide supervision and activities until lone parents get back from work.

Key points

+ The Child Support Agency has a responsibility to make sure an absent parent contributes to the upkeep of his or her child.
+ Lone-parent families are often in need of financial support.
+ The Welfare to Work Scheme is an initiative to encourage lone parents to return to work.
+ The personal social services try to meet the needs of vulnerable families.

Key tasks

1 How can the personal social services help meet the needs of vulnerable families?
2 Explain the role of the Child Support Agency.
3 Describe the types of benefits available to lone-parent families.

Voluntary agencies

Other agencies that provide support to families are voluntary organizations. They are non-profit making bodies that are set up to help and support individuals and families. Voluntary organizations:

+ often work with local authorities to provide a mixture of welfare provision
+ can help meet the needs of the family when they cannot be met by the statutory services
+ can respond quickly in times of urgent or emergency need
+ have staff who are committed and have specific experience.

The role of voluntary agencies

Voluntary agencies can help and support families in the community in a number of different ways.

Direct assistance

Direct assistance means giving practical and physical help to children and families in need. The National Society for Prevention of Cruelty to Children (NSPCC) is an important voluntary organization that works with the social services to support children and families in a number of different ways. Another example of direct assistance is the provision of soft playroom equipment for children with special needs as part of the Children in Need campaign.

Advice and counselling

Some agencies which offer advice and counselling, helping individuals and families in particular situations are:

+ **Citizens Advice Bureau** offers help and advice to families about a wide range of issues, from debt management to access to welfare benefits
+ **ChildLine** offers confidential support and advice for children through a free telephone and website service
+ **Parents Anonymous** offers information, support and help for parents or carers and families.

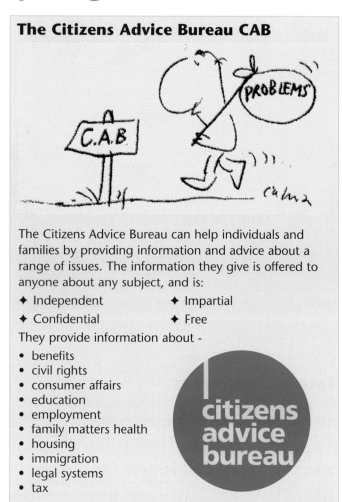

The Citizens Advice Bureau CAB

The Citizens Advice Bureau can help individuals and families by providing information and advice about a range of issues. The information they give is offered to anyone about any subject, and is:

+ Independent   + Impartial
+ Confidential   + Free

They provide information about -

- benefits
- civil rights
- consumer affairs
- education
- employment
- family matters health
- housing
- immigration
- legal systems
- tax

Reproduced with permission of the National Association of Citizens Advice Bureaux

Self-help groups

Individuals and families with the same concerns group together to support and share problems. **Gingerbread** is a support organization for lone-parent families that offers practical help, contact and information.

Pressure groups

These are voluntary groups set up to actively bring about change. **Shelter** campaigns on behalf of the homeless and those in poverty without a decent standard of living. **Child Poverty Action Group** promotes action for the relief of poverty among children and families.

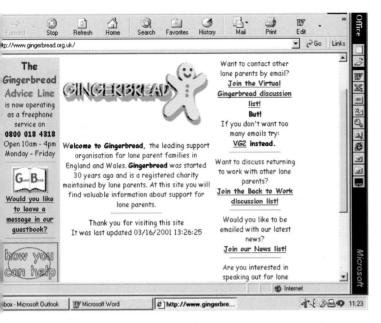

Website of the Gingerbread organization

Non-profit making groups

These groups usually provide a service to the community and although they are often run as a business they do not make a profit – all money generated is used to invest in the service provided. For example, the Women's Royal Voluntary Service (WRVS), which provides a number of services to the community such as the Meals on Wheels service for the elderly and shop facilities at local hospitals.

Council for Voluntary Service

In each local area or town, the Council for Voluntary Service is the agency that will co-ordinate the activities of the voluntary agencies with the local authority services. They play a key role in trying to match community needs with the voluntary and statutory provision available. The role of the local Council for Voluntary Services includes:

+ co-ordinating local voluntary groups such as the WRVS and Citizens Advice Bureau
+ liaising with the local authority social services
+ recruiting and placing volunteers
+ helping to provide resources for voluntary groups
+ sharing of information
+ identifying areas of local need
+ acting as a pressure group to lobby for needs of the community.

Informal care

'Informal care' is the term used to describe the type of care given by relatives, friends and neighbours to help and support families. A carer is anyone who gives time and energy looking after a friend or relative who is ill or disabled. A very large proportion of community care is provided informally in this way. For example, a family who has a child with **Down's syndrome** may need extra help – this is provided by informal carers who are family friends.

For further reference

Most voluntary agencies provide information services on the internet and any search engine can be used to access this information. For example, information about the Child Poverty Action Group can be found by searching for its name or by entering its website address (www.cpag.org.uk)

Key points

+ Voluntary agencies often work with the statutory services to provide a mixture of care.
+ Voluntary agencies can help families in a number of ways such as direct assistance, advice and counselling, self-help groups, pressure groups and non-profit making groups.
+ The Council for Voluntary Service co-ordinates local voluntary groups.
+ Informal care is the care given voluntarily by family, friends and neighbours to help and support individuals and families in need.

Key tasks

1 Explain the different types of voluntary agencies.
2 How are voluntary services in the local area co-ordinated?
3 What is an informal carer?

Further work
Identify a voluntary agency that works with children and find out more about their role. Present your findings in the form of a short report. (RT/IT)

Special needs children

A child with special needs requires additional help and support to live a fulfilling life. A child has special needs if:

+ the child has a disability
+ the child has a learning difficulty that leads to greater learning problems than experienced by most children
+ the child's health or development is impaired in some way (e.g. if his or her physical development is below average for a child of the same age).

Children with disabilities share the same basic needs as other children, but the disability or special need may mean they have additional needs.

Congenital disability

Some disabilities are described as congenital, which means they are present at birth. Some causes of congenital disability include:

+ genetic – where the genetic material inherited from the parents affects the child, e.g. Down's syndrome, haemophilia and muscular dystrophy
+ brain damage – caused before or during the birth of the baby and often a result of a lack of oxygen to the baby (this is known as anoxia). **Cerebral palsy** is a congenital condition caused by lack of oxygen shortly before or during birth
+ developmental – where physical development of the foetus is affected during pregnancy. This could be caused by the mother drinking excessive alcohol, smoking or taking drugs. Diseases such as German measles contracted during pregnancy can also lead to failure of development such as cleft palate or deafness.

Specific disabilities

Physical disability

This is where the disability is related to physical problems such as mobility or co-ordination. This can include:

+ sensory impairment such as blindness or deafness
+ **spina bifida** – a congenital condition that affects 25 in every 1000 births. The baby is

Down's syndrome is a congenital disability

born without a fully formed spine. Surgery can often help children overcome some of the mobility problems
+ cerebral palsy – the area of the brain that controls muscle function is damaged at birth. Children with cerebral palsy have difficulty in controlling their fine manipulative and gross motor movements.

Other disabilities include:

+ emotional difficulties where children have problems relating to others, such as **autism**
+ learning difficulties, which may be a result of a congenital condition such as Down's syndrome
+ behavioral problems, where children can be withdrawn, aggressive or hyperactive – this includes conditions such as **attention deficit disorder**.

Autistic children

Autistic children find it difficult to communicate with others including their families. Most autistic children have difficulties:

+ with speech and language – they are unable to communicate in the usual way, even though they are able to repeat words and phrases
+ with social interaction – children with autism find it difficult to make relationships with their peers, and they find it difficult to understand and respond to other children.

Autism is four times more likely to occur in boys than girls. Three-quarters of children with autism also have learning difficulties.

Children with Down's syndrome

Down's syndrome is a condition that affects 1 in every 1000 babies born. It occurs in children from all cultural, religious and ethnic groups. It is a genetic condition caused by having an extra chromosome in the body's cells. This chromosome disrupts the development of the cells, producing different physical characteristics, such as eyes that slant upwards and outwards. Down's syndrome children also have learning difficulties, which means they have more problems learning than other children of the same age. The chance of having a Down's syndrome child increases with age, particularly if the woman is over the 35 (see table below).

Risk and maternal age – the chance of having a baby with Down's syndrome

Age of mother (years)	Risk
25	1 in 1400
30	1 in 800
35	1 in 380
40	1 in 110
45	1 in 30

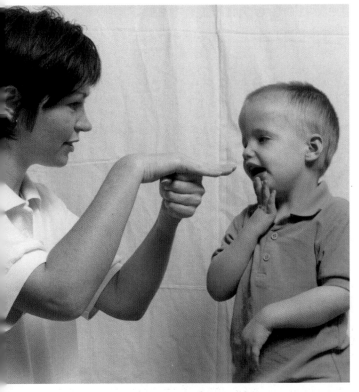

Extra support and help is needed for special needs children

Equal opportunities and special needs

All children should have equal opportunities and entitlement to learning. Current practice in caring for special needs children is based on identifying the needs of the individual child, because all children have different needs. A child who is physically immobile may have highly developed intellectual skills but will need help and support with mobility. The physical immobility may slow down the social development of the child, as it limits the child from gaining independence. For some young special needs children, a little extra support and help is all they need to make progress. Other special needs children may have severe disabilities and need more special help and care.

For further reference

The Children's Act (1989) encourages the integration of special needs children into mainstream nurseries and schools. This is called inclusive care and education.

Key points

✦ A child with special needs requires help and support to live a fulfilling life.
✦ A congenital disability is one that is present at birth.
✦ Down's syndrome is a congenital disability.
✦ Autistic children find it difficult to communicate with others.
✦ All children should have equal opportunities to education.

Key tasks

1 Explain the term 'special needs'.
2 What are the causes of congenital disability?
3 Explain the type of support that is available to families with special needs children.

Further work

Find out what voluntary support services are available in your local area for special needs families. (RT/IT)

Caring for special needs children

Families with children with special needs are entitled to a range of statutory benefits and support.

Support services for families with special needs children

All children have basic needs, and families with special needs children require extra help and support. Local authorities assess these children to identify their needs to make sure help and support is available. Statutory provision for the special needs child and their families includes access to benefits, housing and social services.

Benefits

Benefits include:

+ attendance allowance for children over two years old who need constant care
+ mobility allowance for children unable to move around independently
+ financial help with transport to hospital and school.

Housing

Priority in housing is given to families with special needs children. Local authorities will often adapt the housing to suit the needs of the child, such as widening doorways for wheelchairs and making entry ramps. Specially designed mobility aids can be provided and fitted in the home.

Social services

Social workers can help and support families to ensure they are aware of the services available to them. This means, for example, giving advice on access to benefits, education, local services and to professionals such as speech therapists.

Voluntary agencies

There are a number of voluntary agencies that support special needs children and their families. Most of these agencies are financed by fundraising, although some receive government help. The Royal Society for Mentally Handicapped Adults and Children (MENCAP) is an example of one of these agencies. It is a national organization, with branches in most local areas, which raises money to support their work in the community. Voluntary agencies can help special needs families by:

+ giving specialist information
+ offering practical help and support for the families
+ working with the statutory services to make sure families receive help
+ bringing together families of children with similar problems
+ providing **respite care**.

Respite care

Respite care is a support system that enables families of special needs children to have a break from caring for their child. Many voluntary agencies offer respite care.

Learning opportunities

The developmental progress of a special needs child is influenced by the opportunities he or she is given. His or her progress may be at a different rate to other children. Learning programmes which are designed to speed up the development of children with special needs in the pre-school years are known as **early intervention programmes**.

Early intervention programmes can stimulate a child's learning

They can include specific treatments such as speech therapy and physiotherapy, as well as learning programmes where a trained support worker comes into the home or education setting to work with the child. Many special needs children attend their local school, where a support assistant in the classroom makes sure they have the extra help and support to ensure they make progress.

Playgroups offer opportunities for social and emotional development

Opportunity playgroups

Opportunity playgroups are specialist playgroups for children with special needs. They provide learning opportunities to stimulate and challenge the special needs child. In such playgroups children with special needs can:

✦ join in some or all of the activities with the help of a carer or support assistant
✦ receive specialist help and support from trained professionals to help trigger their developmental progress.

Toys

Toys for special needs children should be chosen to match the child's stage of development rather than his or her age. For example, a toy that involves posting shapes through holes in a box will suit a child whose hand–eye co-ordination allows them to grasp the object and push it through the hole, regardless of his or her age or ability in other areas of development.

Families

Most special needs children live at home with their families. The special needs child presents families with many challenges. The physical care of the child may be very demanding, and there may be insensitivity from others in the community. However, there are many positive effects – family bonds become stronger as everyone works to care for and support the special needs child.

Attitudes in society

People react in different ways to children with special needs. Some avoid contact because they are embarrassed, whereas others are overprotective. It is important that the lives of all children are valued, and that special needs children have equal opportunities and enjoy the same rights.

Key points

✦ Families with children who have special needs are entitled to a range of statutory benefits and support.
✦ Statutory provision for the special needs child and his or her family includes access to additional benefits, housing and social services.
✦ Respite care is a support system that enables families of special needs children to have a break from caring for their child.
✦ Early intervention programmes help speed the developmental progress of the pre-school special needs child.

Key tasks

1 Explain the range of support services available to families with special needs children.
2 How can an opportunity playgroup help the development of a special needs child?
3 What does the term 'equal opportunities' mean?

Further work	Identify a charity that works to help and support special needs children and their families. Find out the range of information and support that they provide. (RT/IT)

Child safety

Accidents are the most common cause of death in children over the age of one. Children have accidents because they are not aware of the dangers in their environment. This means safety is a major responsibility for parents and carers.

Accident statistics

Accident statistics show the number and types of accident that happen. Children under five are most at risk from accidents. The most serious accidents in the home happen on the stairs or in the kitchen.

The table below shows that falls are the cause of almost half of non-fatal accidents.

Non-fatal accidents in the home to children under five years of age

Type of accident	Number of accidents	Percentage %
Falls	230 000	48
Struck	111 000	23
Foreign body	36 000	8
Poisoning	32 000	7
Thermal/burn	31 000	6
Cuts	26 000	5
Bites/stings	12 000	3

Source: RoSPA, 1998

These statistics are for accidents where children are injured, but more than 100 young children die every year from fatal accidents in the home. House fires are the most common cause of accidental death in the home to children under five.

For further reference

The Royal Society for Prevention of Accidents (RoSPA) is a charitable organization that provides an information service to promote home safety and prevent accidents. Visit their website at www.rospa.co.uk

Safety and developmental stages

Babies and children will be more at risk from particular hazards at different stages in their development. A hazard is a potential danger, such as a hot drink or a sharp edge on a toy.

Link: *For more information on physical development see pages 34–47.*

Newborn babies should never be left alone on raised surfaces as they could roll over and fall off.

Six-month-old babies put anything in their mouths that they can grasp. As soon as babies start to move about and explore, the chance of accident increases.

Toddlers learn to develop their skills of locomotion. They try to balance and climb up on objects.

Three-year-olds are adventurous and want to explore and test their skills.

Four-year-olds are more independent and keen to try activities such as riding a bike or swinging on a rope.

Parents and carers

Parents and carers need to be aware of the potential dangers for their child at different stages of development. When the child is ready, parents and carers need to make them aware of these dangers. Very young children cannot understand danger. It is not until a child is two that it can start to understand how some actions have consequences, such as if they touch a hot iron it will hurt. Helping the child learn about dangers around him or her without stopping his or her natural curiosity and growing independence is a difficult balance to achieve.

Why children have accidents

Children have accidents because:

+ they are often absorbed in activities and unaware of the danger in their surroundings
+ they lack experience and do not understand the consequences of what they do
+ they are naturally curious and inquisitive – this can often lead them into danger
+ they are small and often cannot see the hazards around them which are obvious to adults
+ if they are overexcited or emotionally upset they are more likely to have accidents.

Other risk factors include:

+ supervision – many accidents happen when children are not supervised
+ time of day – more accidents happen in the late afternoon or evening, in the summer or at weekends
+ gender – boys are more likely to have accidents than girls
+ emotional factors and stress such as illness or death in the family increase the likelihood of having an accident.

Dangers can be explained to a two-year-old

Fewer accidents happen when children are supervised

Key tasks

1 Explain the reasons why children under five have more accidents than older children.
2 Describe how parents and carers can help their children to be aware of potential hazards.
3 Explain why babies and young children are more at risk from particular hazards at different stages in their development.

Further work	Using ICT, produce a pie or bar chart to show the percentage of non-fatal accidents by type. (RT/IT)

Accident prevention

Accidents can be prevented. No home or garden can be made totally accident-proof, but an awareness of the most likely hazards can reduce the risk of accidents (see table below).

Accident prevention in the home

Accidental injury	Hazard	Prevention
Falls	Falling down stairs and steps, rolling off surfaces, falling out of cots/prams/buggies, falling out of windows	Use of safety gates and window locks, ensure stair area is well lit, teach safe way to climb stairs, supervision of activity sessions
Choking and suffocation	Objects put in child's mouth, choking on food and suffocation by plastic bags	Always supervise a young child when they are eating, keep small objects such as buttons out of reach, store plastic bags safely
Cuts	Sharp tools left out, broken glass, sharp edges to objects in the home	Keep sharp tools out of reach, use safety glass or safety (shatter resistant) film on vulnerable doors, such as patio doors
Electrocution	Poking objects into plug sockets, handling electrical equipment, unsafe electrical equipment	Use socket guards, regularly check safety of electrical equipment, teach children dangers of electricity when they are old enough to understand
Scalds and burns	Hot surfaces in the kitchen, hot liquids in kettles, fires, hot water in bath	Supervise children closely in kitchen area, take particular care with hot drinks, use cooker guards and fireguards, test temperature of bath water
Poisoning	Household chemicals such as bleach, tablets and medications, alcohol accessible to child	Keep all household chemicals in original, labelled container, securely stored, keep medicines stored in a locked cabinet and store alcohol safely out of reach
Drowning	Child left alone in bath, uncovered bowls or buckets of liquid in the home, unsupervised access to paddling pools and ponds	Children must always be supervised as they can drown in just a few centimetres of water

Creating a safe environment for children

Hazards can be identified and action can be taken to prevent accidents in the home. Serious accidents often happen in the kitchen.

fitting a smoke alarm and checking it regularly

storing sharp tools safely in cupboards out of reach of children

using a cooker guard to prevent the child reaching pans

ensuring electrical flexes are secure and out of reach

storing plastic bags carefully

ensuring no objects are stored on the floor which could be tripped over

using a non-slip floor surface

ensuring domestic chemicals such as cleaning agents are stored in a locked cupboard

Actions that can be taken to make a kitchen area safe

First aid

All small children will have minor accidents as they grow up, so it is important that all homes have a basic first aid box which parents or carers can use.

Hazardous substances

Every year almost 10 000 children are rushed to hospital because they have swallowed a **hazardous substance**. Most of these hazardous substances are common household chemicals such as bleach, anti-freeze, aftershave or lavatory cleaner. Children under the age of five are naturally curious, and like exploring and investigating brightly coloured and unusually

Domestic chemicals should be stored in a locked cupboard

shaped containers. Hazardous substances are labelled clearly to show parents and carers the dangers (see table below).

Warning labels on hazardous household chemicals

Label	Description of substance
Harmful/irritant	A substance that is not a serious health risk but may cause some ill health if it is inhaled, swallowed or spilt on the skin. Some of these substances may irritate the eyes and skin
Toxic/very toxic	Can cause serious risk to health if swallowed and in some cases if inhaled or spilt on the skin
Corrosive	May cause painful burns and destroys body tissue

Reducing the risks

The risks are reduced as follows:

✦ over half of the accidental poisonings happen when children are left on their own for less than five minutes
young children should not be left unsupervised

✦ children are attracted by the colour and shape of containers
keep all household chemicals out of sight and out of reach of children

✦ many of the accidents with household chemicals happen to children under three years of age
remember that children of this age cannot understand the dangers

✦ accidents can happen if hazardous substances are stored in a different container
always store products in their original containers.

For further reference

Most household chemicals and medicines have **child-resistant closures** that are used to prevent or delay the child opening the product. Medicines used in the home are also a hazard to children – they are attractive because of their colour and shape.

Key points

✦ An awareness of the most likely hazards can reduce the risk of accidents.
✦ Young children should never be left unsupervised.
✦ Serious accidents often happen in the kitchen.
✦ All homes should have a basic first aid box for parents or carers to use.
✦ Many household chemicals are hazardous.
✦ Keep all household chemicals out of sight and out of reach of children.

Key task

Look at the actions that can be taken to make the kitchen safer. Identify each of the hazards and explain the type of accidental injury that would be caused if the action was not taken.

Further work

1 Design a poster to show the dangers of common household substances which could be used in your local health centre. (RT/IT)

2 Choose a room where toddlers play and identify the possible safety hazards. Suggest possible actions that could be taken to prevent accidents. Display the information you have gathered in a table like the one below. (RT/IT)

Hazard identified	Action to be taken

Safety outside the home

Playing outside

The garden is seen as a safe place for children to play, but there are a number of hazards that exist. Young children should be supervised when they are playing outside in the garden.

Gardens may contain many hazards for young children

Hazards may include:

+ poisonous plants such as laburnum
+ bacteria from animal faeces
+ water (children can drown in just a few inches)
+ rusty and broken objects
+ access to roads through broken fences.

Play equipment

Play and adventure areas are very exciting places for children under the age of five to explore. These areas are designed with safety in mind. The British Standard for play equipment is BS 5696. Regulations relating to playground equipment is complex but they include key points such as:

+ all swings should have rubber seats to soften the impact if they hit a child
+ swings for younger children should have cradle seats
+ slides should be set in slopes or banks
+ floor areas should be made of materials that cushion falls, such as bark chippings
+ there should be plenty of space between play equipment, and play areas should be fenced off.

Adventure playgrounds can help children develop their physical skills and develop growing independence as they are encouraged to test themselves in activities. They are

appropriate for children of the right age, but parents and carers have to decide at what age a child is ready to try out his or her skills.

Play equipment helps children develop their physical skills

Road safety

The number of under fives killed or seriously injured in accidents when playing on or near roads has fallen over the last ten years. However, in the United Kingdom these figures are still higher than the rest of Europe.

The government 'Kill your speed' campaign was set up to reduce the number of children being killed or injured on or near roads. Young children are particularly at risk because:

+ they do not understand the dangers
+ they cannot judge the speed or distance of traffic
+ their size makes it difficult for them to have a good view of traffic.

The Green Cross Code

This is a system designed to help children understand how to cross the road safely in today's traffic. The code teaches the child to follow a simple procedure to cross the road safely. Children under five years should never be out alone, and should learn safety rules by example every time they are out with parents and carers. Children aged five or under cannot assess the speed of cars or understand the danger. The first stage of the Green Cross Code is to teach children to:

+ stop
+ look all around for traffic
+ listen for traffic before they cross the road.

Five-year-olds may learn the Green Cross Code, but may not understand it. They should not be expected to follow the code on their own. It is only when the child is older, at about seven years of age, that he or she will be able to follow and understand the rules of the Green Cross Code.

Children learn by example

Travelling safely by car

The law states that all children who travel in a car must be in a **safety restraint**. Injuries to children in car accidents can be reduced by wearing a suitable child restraint or seat belt. There are a wide variety of child restraints depending on the weight, size and age of the child. They are categorized by weight and age guides (0, 0+, 1, 2 and 3) to help parents and carers choose the most appropriate seat for their child (see table). *It is essential that the car seats and restraints are fitted correctly and that the harnesses and straps are adjusted before each journey. It is also essential that car seats are never used in the front seat of a car with air bags because of the risk of suffocation if the bag inflates.* All child seats and restraints must carry a **British Standards kitemark**.

For further reference

The British Standards Institution set standards for a wide range of products related to child safety, from safety gates to seat belts to children's nightwear. For more information visit their website at www.bsi-global.com

Types of child car seat or restraint

Type of restraint	Description
Infant carrier 	Infant carriers are usually fitted rear-facing and are often used to carry babies outside the car. Head huggers are often supplied to support the heads of newborn babies. Carriers are only suitable for babies up to about nine months old and weighing less than 13kg
Child safety seats 	Child safety seats are usually front-facing and fit in the rear of the car. They are suitable for children weighing between 9 and 18kg and can have adjustable positions
Harnesses 	Safety harnesses are used for the older child. They have adjustable waist and shoulder straps and are used with a booster seat to raise the child slightly in the seat

Key points

✦ Gardens can contain many hazards for young children.
✦ The Green Cross Code is a system to help children understand how to cross the road safely.
✦ All children who travel in a car must be in a safety restraint.
✦ All child restraints must carry a British Standards kitemark.

Key tasks

1 Explain why young children have so many road accidents.
2 Design an informative poster to help a five-year-old child understand the Green Cross Code.

Further work	Visit a children's play area and explain whether you think it is a safe place for children to play. (RT/IT)

Safety issues

Child-related products

It is essential that products that are used with children are safe. Consumer law such as The General Product Safety Regulations (1994) makes sure that manufacturers of products comply with the standards set down by the government. Some products where safety is an important factor, such as pushchairs, also have to conform to a British Standard.

The British Standards kitemark

The kitemark of the British Standards Institution is found on a wide range of products and equipment used by children, such as safety gates, car seats, pushchairs and electrical equipment. The British Standards Institute check the product against an agreed standard to make sure it will perform its job properly and safely. Their tests judge the quality and suitability of the materials the product is made out of, as well as the safety and design features of the product.

The toy safety code

British Standards kitemark

Toy safety

Playing with toys is an essential part of every child's development, but toys are involved in about 30 000 accidents every year. A safe toy is one that does not harm the child in any way. Toys are designed for a specific age of child to match their stage of development.

Toys used by children at the wrong age could cause a hazard. For example, a nine-month-old baby playing with small plastic dice could swallow and choke on the dice. Toys should be kept in a clean condition, particularly those for young babies who put everything in their mouths. They should be regularly checked to make sure they have no loose parts and no sharp edges to harm a child.

Toys and the law

The Toys (Safety) Regulations (1995) makes sure that toys that are sold in the United Kingdom are safe. To comply with the law, toys are tested in many ways. For example, there is a test to check that the materials the toys are made out of are safe. Textiles used to make toys, both in the outside construction and the filling, should be non-flammable. Plastics, metals and paints used must be non-toxic.

When buying toys for children, look for the following symbols on the product:

The European Community symbol shows that the toy meets the standards of the Toy Safety Directive

The CE 'lion' mark is found on toys made in the United Kingdom and shows that the toy meets the safety requirements of the British Toy Manufacturers Association

Safety of children's nightwear

The Nightwear (Safety) Regulations states that all children's nightwear must pass a test for slow burning fabrics. Any children's clothes made from terry towelling, which can be very flammable, must carry a permanent label to show whether the clothes have passed the low flammability test.

> **LOW FLAMMABILITY TO BS 5722**

> **KEEP AWAY FROM FIRE**

Clothing safety

If the 'keep away from fire' label is on an item of children's clothing, extreme care is needed as the fabric the clothes are made from is not slow burning

Many children's clothes are bought by mail order – the labels for mail order clothes look different but mean exactly the same thing

Labels found on children's mail order clothes

If parents and carers make nightwear for children themselves, they should choose a low flammability fabric. Nylon and polyester are safer than cottons and cotton mixtures. Any thread and trimmings used should also be low flammability.

Personal safety

National campaigns to promote the personal safety of children, such as the 'Say no' campaign, have raised the awareness of the community to child safety. Safety has become more of an issue today as many parents and carers spend time away from their children while at work and entrust their care to others. Parents and carers today worry about their children being abducted. This happens very rarely, but it is sensible for young children to be given simple guidelines about how to cope if they should ever find themselves on their own. These could include:

+ never going with anyone they do not know
+ letting their parents or carers know if they are approached by anyone
+ if lost, wait and stand still until they are found.

Summary of child safety

All children have accidents regardless of the actions taken by parents and carers to prevent them. Young children cannot concentrate on more than one thing at a time – if a child is playing with a ball and it rolls in the road they will think about chasing the ball not the danger of the road.

Children need to explore as part of their growing independence, and parents and carers need to allow children this opportunity but in a safe, supervised environment. Accidents can be prevented by:

+ parents and carers being aware of safety hazards
+ parents and carers taking action to improve the safety of the child's environment
+ ensuring young children are adequately supervised
+ setting good examples of appropriate behaviour by adults
+ improving the design and labelling of products related to child safety.

Key tasks

1 Describe the safety points that are important when choosing toys for children.
2 Explain why young children are more likely to have accidents than older children.
3 How does the British Standards Institute test products to make sure they are safe?

Further work	Carry out a survey of toys or nightwear for the young baby to find out if the products are correctly labelled. (RT/IT)

Parenthood and pregnancy

1 a Name the three methods of contraception shown in the pictures below.

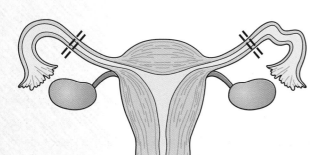

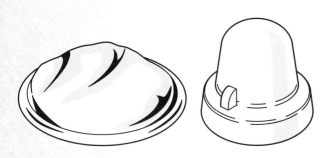

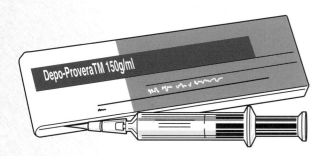

b Study the table below and answer the questions that follow.

Name of contraceptive	How it works	How reliable it is
Combined pill	This type of pill contains two hormones, oestrogen and progestrogen, which stop the ovaries from producing eggs	Almost 100 per cent reliable if taken according to instructions
Male condom	A tube made of thin rubber, closed at one end, which is fitted over the erect penis before intercourse takes place. It prevents sperm from getting into the woman's vagina	With careful use only about two women in 100 will become pregnant
IUD (intrauterine device), coil or loop	A small plastic and copper device is placed into the uterus. It works mainly by stopping a fertilized egg from settling in the uterus	About two women in every 100 will become pregnant

i Name the two hormones that are found in the combined pill.
ii How reliable is the combined pill?
iii Name the method of contraception that prevents sperm from entering the vagina.
iv Give another name for IUD.

c Describe the advantages and disadvantages of the following contraceptive methods:
i Femidom.
ii IUS.
iii NFP.

Ovulation occurs
around day 14

| 1 | 2 | 3 | 4 | 5 | 6 | 7 | 8 | 9 | 10 | 11 | 12 | 13 | 14 | 15 | 16 | 17 | 18 | 19 | 20 | 21 | 22 | 23 | 24 | 25 | 26 | 27 | 28 |

Menstruation – day 1-5
Lining of the uterus grows – day 6-15
Uterus is ready to receive an egg – day 16-21
Lining of uterus starts to break down – day 22-28

2 a Study the diagram above and answer the questions that follow.
   i How many days is menstruation taking place?
   ii On what day is ovulation likely to take place?
   iii After ovulation, what is the uterus ready to receive?
   iv How many days on average does the menstrual cycle take to complete?

  b Where in the female reproductive system does fertilization take place?

  c Explain the following terms.
   i Ovulation.
   ii Fertilization.
   iii Implantation.

3 a Give three signs that indicate that a woman has gone into labour.

  b Look at the pictures below of a baby being born and explain what is happening in each of them.

  c What is an episiotomy?

  d Explain why forceps may be used during labour.

4 Antenatal care is available to all pregnant women. Explain what takes place at each of the following:

a An antenatal clinic.

b An antenatal class.

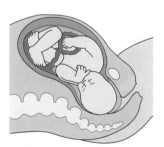
Stage 1

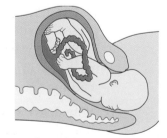
Stage 2

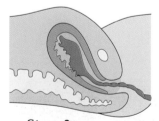
Stage 3

Physical development

1 a i Suggest two reasons why babies may cry.

   ii What advice would you give to a parent or carer to help stop a baby from crying?

  b What is a reflex action?

  c Complete the following table on reflex actions.

Reflex action	Stimulus (cause of movement)	Response (movement that follows)
Sucking reflex	Something is put into mouth	Baby immediately sucks
Grasp reflex		
	Gently touching the baby's cheek	
		Baby clenches hands and moves arms outwards with elbows bent

  d Describe each of the following:
   i Vernix.
   ii Fontanelle.

2 a What do you understand by the term 'physical development'?

  b Look at the following pictures. Describe the stages of physical development shown and give an approximate age for each one.

  c What do you understand by the term 'fine manipulative skills'?

  d Suggest three ways a parent or carer could encourage these skills in a six-month-old baby.

3 a Why is it important that children have an established routine?

  b Describe what is meant by a 'regular sleep pattern'.

  c How can a parent or carer help a child to become toilet trained?

  d Why does the housing environment play an important part in a child's development?

4 a i Explain the meaning of the term 'premature baby'.
   ii What difficulties may premature babies have?
   iii Explain the value of an incubator for a premature baby.

  b i Explain the term 'cot death'.
   ii What advice would you give to a parent or carer to help prevent cot death?

Nutrition and health

1 a Give four reasons why breast milk is considered by doctors to be the best milk for babies.

   b Why do some mothers choose to bottle feed their babies?

2 Extra care needs to be taken to prevent food poisoning in young children. Explain how food poisoning can be avoided in the home.

3 The chart below is taken from a packet of formula milk powder.

Approx. age of baby	Approx. weight in kg	Approx. weight in lbs	Level scoops of feed
Birth	3.5	7.5	3
2 weeks	4.0	8.8	4
2 months	5.0	11.0	6
4 months	6.5	14.5	7
6 months	7.5	16.5	8

   a i How many level scoops of feed is needed for a baby aged two weeks?

      ii How much liquid is needed for a baby of four months?

      iii How many feeds in 24 hours should a baby of two weeks be given?

   b Explain why it is important to measure the amount of formula feed accurately.

   c Describe how to make up a bottle of formula milk.

4 Parents can usually tell when their child is ill.

   a Suggest three symptoms which would tell parents or carers their child was ill.

   b Identify and describe three infectious diseases of childhood.

   c Describe how to care for a toddler who is ill.

5 Weaning is the term used to explain how a young child moves from liquid to solid food.

   a At what age does a young child begin weaning?

   b What signs do babies give that they are ready to start weaning?

   c What advice could be given to a mother about suitable foods to start a baby weaning?

6 A range of prepared baby food products are available in tins, jars and packets.

   a Suggest three reasons why a parent or carer may use these food products.

   b Explain how the label on the baby food product could help inform the parent.

7 Many working mothers decide to bottle feed their baby.

   a Explain the advantages of bottle feeding for the working parent.

   b Suggest why care needs to be taken when preparing bottle feeds for babies.

8 Immunization helps protect a child from disease.

   a Explain how infection is spread.

   b Describe how immunization prevents a child getting the disease.

   c Explain why some parents are reluctant to get their child immunized.

Intellectual, social and emotional development

1 a What do you understand by the term 'intellectual development'?

b What is meant by the term 'nature and nurture'?

c Suggest four conditions that are necessary for a child to develop intellectually.

d Children learn by using a number of different factors.
   i Name three of these factors.
   ii Explain how each factor will help a child to learn.

2 a What do you understand by the term 'emotional development'?

b Why is bonding so important between a baby and its parents or carers?

c Explain how a parent or carer may help a child to overcome any jealousy felt when a new baby arrives in the family.

d Babies and young children often have some form of comforter.
   i Suggest an idea for a comforter.
   ii Why do babies and children sometimes need to have comforters?

3 a What do you understand by the term 'social development'?

b Explain how the following would have an effect on a child's social development.
   i Living in a remote area.
   ii Coming from a wealthy family.
   iii Being an only child.

c i Why is social play so important in a child's development?
   ii Give three examples of social play.

4 a Study the table below, which from a toy shop catalogue.

Approximate age of child	Suitable toys
Up to six months	Choose toys to encourage skills such as eye movement, listening and grasping, e.g. teething rings, a musical mobile, soft toys and an activity gym
Six to twelve months	Choose toys to encourage hand movements, hand–eye co-ordination and exploring with hand and mouth, e.g. a bell rattle, activity centre and pull-along toys
One to two years	Choose toys to encourage fine manipulative skills, and balance and mobility, e.g. building blocks, push-and-pull toys, posting box
Two to five years	Choose toys to encourage and develop all physical skills, e.g. construction toys, peg boards, and chalkboards and chalk

   i Name a skill that needs to be encouraged in a child up to the age of six months.
   ii Suggest a toy that is suitable for a child aged six to twelve months.
   iii Name a skill that needs to be developed in a child aged one to two years.
   iv Suggest a toy that is suitable for a child aged two to five years.

b Explain the following terms.
   i Role-play.
   ii Sensory exploration.

c What is meant by the following terms?
   i Non-verbal communication.
   ii Verbal communication.

d Children learn at different rates. Give four reasons for these variations.

The family and the community

1   a   Suggest three reasons why children are taken into local authority care.

    b   Sometimes children do not live with their natural parents and are cared for by foster or adoptive parents. Explain the terms fostering and adoption.

2   Many women choose to work and to use a registered child minder to look after their children.

    a   Identify the points a parent or carer should look for when choosing a child minder for their child.

    b   Describe how the local authority checks the quality of provision offered by child minders.

3   a   Give two examples of types of pre-school groups for young children.

    b   Explain the ways pre school education helps with a child's early education.

4   There has been an increase in the number of lone parents families.

    a   Explain the term 'lone-parent family'.

    b   Suggest reasons for the increase in the number of lone parent families.

    c   Identify the benefits that are available to support the lone-parent family.

5   Family structures in society are changing.

    a   Describe the structure of:
      i   nuclear family.
      ii   extended family.
      iii reconstituted family.

    b   Explain the reasons why family structures are changing.

6   Many children under five are not cared for by their parents during the day.

    a   Explain why there is a need for day care provision.

    b   Describe the types of day care provision available for pre-school children.

7   There are many benefits of a young child attending a pre-school group. Explain how the following children would benefit:

    a   a child who lives in a small flat.

    b   an only child.

    c   a child from a low income family.

8   Many families have children with special needs.

    a   Describe the statutory support available to families with special needs children.

    b   Explain how voluntary agencies can help these families care for their special needs child.

About the coursework

As part of your Child Development for OCR GCSE, you have to complete three pieces of coursework for the internal assessment component. These pieces should comprise:

+ one individual task
+ two resource tasks.

These pieces of coursework count for up to 50 per cent of your final mark. You will also have to sit an exam at the end of your course, which also counts for up to 50 per cent of your final mark. You should try to present your coursework using a range of methods, including the use of ICT where appropriate.

Your individual task should take approximately twelve to fourteen hours to complete and each resource task should take approximately two to three hours to complete.

The individual task

This piece of coursework carries 30 per cent of the total marks available. It involves investigation and problem-solving skills, and must include the observation of a child or children. Before starting this task, it is useful to have already had experience of children and to have spent some time observing them. You should already have covered some of the content of the course, e.g. physical, social, intellectual and emotional development before you start your individual task. Before carrying out your individual task, you should already have done some resource tasks to develop your skills of research and investigation.

Selection of the individual task title

The individual task title will be developed during the task analysis section (see page 129). It is vital that you develop and produce your own task title in order to meet the assessment criteria. If you have difficulty achieving this without help, your teacher can offer you support and guidance.

The resource tasks

The resource tasks are pieces of coursework that are short and focused on an area of the subject content. Each resource task carries ten per cent of the total mark available. A number of resource tasks may be carried out but only two are selected for the final assessment (twenty per cent of the final mark).

Selection of the resource task titles

The resource task titles will be set by your teacher, and should be relevant to the subject content being taught. The amount of time to be spent on each task will be laid down by your teacher, so you should be aware of how much time you should spend on each area. However, you do not need to record these timings in your resource tasks.

To conclude, individual and resource tasks require a number of skills (see diagram below).

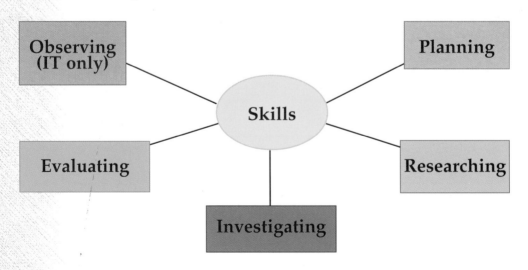

Individual task: task analysis

The task analysis stage involves the research into the child/children to be studied and the area(s) of development chosen to be studied. It is important that when the research has been carried out, a worthwhile task title is selected. You should work through the following stages.

1 Consider the background information of the child/children

This is the initial research carried out to provide information about the child/children to be studied, e.g. age, position in the family, type of house, likes and dislikes. It is important to recognize that the confidentiality of the child is vital, so no surnames or addresses should be included. The stages of development that the child has acquired so far should also be included, i.e. physical, social, emotional, intellectual and language.

2 Consider the appropriate areas of development

To help you choose an appropriate area(s) give a definition of all the areas of development, and link this to the child's developmental progress so that you can see which area(s) of development are the most appropriate.

3 Choose area(s) of interest in the specification relevant to child development

This is where an area or areas of development are chosen. The area needs to be relevant to the age of the child, e.g. intellectual skills would be more appropriate for a four-year-old child but not so for a five-month-old baby because it would not be so easy to collect information from the younger child.

Another example would be physical development. This would be very appropriate for a nine-month-old baby as there is plenty of physical development taking place, but not so for a five-year-old child who has completed most stages of physical development.

More than one area can be chosen if you feel it is appropriate. However, it is more difficult to focus on two or more areas, and careful thought would need to be put into this.

4 Give reasons for choosing the area(s) of development

Once the area(s) of development has been chosen, reasons for the choice need to be given. This should be linked to the child's own development progression.

5 Suggest possible resources

It is important to list some possibilities about where information can be found, e.g. books, videos and leaflets (see diagram below). You do not have to use all of them, but you should consider all the possible resources.

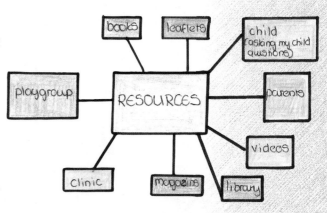

6 Carry out research into the chosen area(s)

It is important to be selective in the research of the area(s) of development and all research should be linked to the age of the child. It is not necessary to cover the whole of the nought to five year age range, e.g. if the child is aged two years it would only be appropriate to provide research on eighteen months to three years on the area(s) of development chosen. This will then allow you to examine, later in the task, if the child is below average, average, or above average in development progress for his or her age. The research can be presented in any form that is appropriate, e.g. bullet points or spider diagrams, and a variety of sources should be encouraged.

7 Write a relevant task title

Once all the research has been collected and presented, the task title can be written (see below). This should be relevant to the child/children and to the area(s) of development chosen. It can be written as a question to answer, or as a hypothesis, or as a statement to evaluate. The rest of the task will then focus around this title.

HOW DO THE FINE MANIPULATIVE ACTIONS OF AN 18 MONTH OLD DEVELOP AND DIFFER ACCORDING TO THE OBJECT?

Task title examples

How a twenty-one-month-old toddler develops physical and manipulative skills.

How do the fine manipulative actions of an eighteen-month-old develop and differ according to the object?

Once the task title has been written, the task analysis section is now complete, but it is important to recognize that all sections of the individual task overlap with each other and they should not be seen and treated as separate.

Individual task: development

It is important to recognize that this section refers to the development of the task. The research that has been collected in the task analysis section now needs to be referred to as the development part of the task is worked through. You should work through the following stages.

1 Use research collected in the task analysis when suggesting ideas and making decisions

You should be aware that it is important to use the research collected and recorded on the chosen area(s) of development in the task analysis when making suggestions and giving reasons for decisions. Using the research will allow you to suggest appropriate and relevant solutions. For example, if you are studying the area of physical development and manipulative skills in a nine-month-old baby, the research will show that a baby of this age is picking up objects using the fingers and thumb. Therefore a suitable activity that could be carried out would be to set out some objects for the baby to pick up. The observation would be to see how the baby is progressing in these manipulative skills. The research also allows you to give relevant reasons why these activities have been chosen.

2 Suggest methods of observing the child/children

You need to suggest a variety of methods of observation that could be carried out to enable the most appropriate methods to be selected (see diagram opposite). It is not necessary for all the suggested methods to be used, as long as they are considered as a possibility. Here are some different methods:

♦ an organized activity set up by you for the child to carry out, e.g. threading beads or painting
♦ an activity that involves you joining in with the child, e.g. throwing and catching a ball
♦ an observation where you may compare the development of two children of a similar age
♦ arriving to observe the child at a certain time, e.g. bathtime or a mealtime
♦ observing the child/children in their familiar surroundings without organizing an activity, e.g. arriving in a morning and observing what the child would normally be doing during the day.

Any other method of observation may also be appropriate and you should explore all the possibilities.

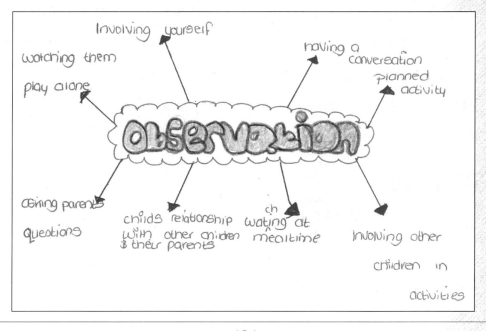

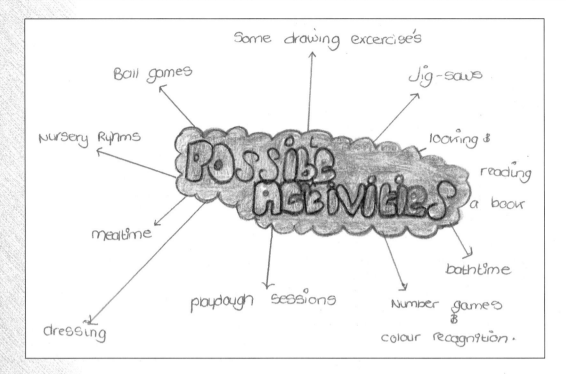

3 Consider possible activities that could be carried out

You need to think about all the possible activities that could be carried out with your child, but you do not necessarily need to carry them all out (see diagram below). The activities suggested must be relevant to the chosen area(s) of development. The research in the task analysis section will enable you to select appropriate solutions and the activities should be linked to this research.

4 Consider the length and frequency of the observations

The timing and the frequency of the observations are important and will depend mostly on the chosen area(s) of development. Once again, you are required to produce possibilities of the timing and the frequency. For example, if the task title is to compare drawing skills in a group of three-year-old children, the observations could be done over a shorter period of time than for a task title that says 'How does a two-year-old's communication skills develop?' where the observations would need to be spread over a longer period of time as language skills develop more slowly. Students must be aware that

children's concentration spans are relatively short, so the timing of the observations should be realistic, e.g. ten or fifteen minutes.

5 Make decisions on which methods and activities are to be used

The observation methods and activities need to be chosen from all the suggestions that have been recorded. Careful consideration should be given and the most appropriate should be selected. For example, if social development is chosen, an appropriate method of observation and activity would be to see how the child behaves and reacts with others around the table at mealtimes.

6 Justify those decisions (i.e. give reasons)

Once the methods and activities have been chosen, reasons should be given about why they were selected using the research in the task analysis section to support these decisions.

As there is a great deal of overlap between the development and the planning sections, these could be covered together.

Individual task: planning

If careful, detailed planning is carried out, it will help ensure that the observations run smoothly and successfully. The planning section is closely linked to the development section, so all decisions that have been made in the development section will now be carried forward and planned in more detail for the observations. You should work through the following stages.

1 Develop a logical plan of action

It will help you if you produce an overview of all the observations to be carried out, showing the order that they are going to be done in. This can be presented in any form, e.g. a simple flow chart (see diagram below). You could use ICT to produce this.

The overview does not require details of each observation, unless you wish to include the next stage as well and cover both stages together. The overview does enable you to focus on the order of the observations.

2 Plan individual observations

Each observation should be planned in detail and should include the following details (see below):

✦ timings – the length of the observation needs to be considered so that you can plan what to do for the decided length of time. Refer to the suggested timings in the development section
✦ methods of observation – these also need to be stated
✦ details about the activity – these need to be planned and you should state what the child/children are going to do. You will also need to say what you are looking for in each activity
✦ resources required – if any resources are needed, these should be put into the plan, e.g. if a painting activity is to be carried out, items such as brushes, paints, aprons and paper will be necessary.

A flow chart to show the order of my activities

1. Undressing activity
2. Communication activity
3. Conversation activity
4. Meal time activity
5. Different atmosphere
6. Dressing activity

Observations

Visit - 1 - My first visit will be a ten minute visit so Amy will get used to me. During the ten minute visit I will play a game of threading beans to make a necklace. I have to ensure that Amy cannot put the beads into her mouth. I will be looking for which hand Amy picks the beads up in, how she threads the beads and how Amy holds the beads.

Visit - 2 - My second visit will be a week after the first visit and it will last for ten minutes. I will build a tower with bricks. I will be observing the type of tower Amy builds, watching which hand Amy picks the bricks up in and how many bricks Amy picks up at a time.

3 Suggest a variety of methods to record the observations

In order to ensure that everything is recorded accurately, and in such a way that you will not miss any developmental progress during an observation, recording strategies need to be considered. These can range from a chart or table (see below) to the use of equipment such as a camera or video recorder. It should also be considered that some activities could provide their own method of recording, e.g. a painting activity will provide a picture that can be used as evidence.

4 Suggest alternative ways to overcome any problems

You need to consider any possible problems that may occur whilst carrying out the observations, and possible solutions should be given. For example, if an activity has been planned outside and it rains on the arranged day, what could be done instead? It would be useful if a variety of problems could be considered as this will help you if any problems arise.

It should be noted that if any changes are made to the plan for whatever reason, these should be noted and recorded in the evaluation section of the individual task.

As there is a great deal of overlap between the development and the planning sections, these could be covered together.

Visit 1

Activity	Did the child use two hands to undress		Did the child start undressing at the top	Comment on any other information
UNDRESSING	YES	NO	YES	
	Did the child undo all the buttons on his clothing		NO	
	YES	NO	Did the child begin undressing from the bottom	
	Did the child find it difficult		YES	
	YES	NO	NO	

Individual task: execution

This area is split into two sections: observations and application of knowledge. However, although they are separate in terms of what is required in each, the information produced can be presented in one form. The application of knowledge can be done within each observation or as a separate section at the end of all the observations. It is a matter of personal preference as to how it is presented. As with the rest of the individual task, use ICT where appropriate. You should work through the following stages.

Observations

You will be credited for the quality of your responses in the observations rather than the quantity. There are no rules as to how many observations should be carried out, but there should be as many as it takes to enable you to collect enough information to fulfil the task title. You should work through the following stages.

1 Observations should be well recorded and detailed accounts

Whatever methods of recording observations are used, e.g. a camera, a video recorder and charts, they should be well documented, providing written evidence as to what took place (see the example). Certain details will provide the necessary information, such as time, place and length of visit, and then a written account should be submitted to support any graphic evidence or to explain information recorded in a chart (see the example). Although it is relevant to set the scene, e.g. to say who is present, do not write anecdotal stories. For example, 'I arrived at Jo's house, talked to Jo's mum and watched Jo playing with his toys. He sat for a few minutes and then went outside to play with a ball.' In this description there is no evidence of any developmental observation.

VISIT 1

Friday 29th Sep

Based at – *Morgans House*

Completion = 8 mins

I found it very difficult doing the undressing activity. Morgan became very irritable by the end. I told Morgan to undress himself, he didn't co-operate. I then began to give Morgan a boost. I showed him what to do. After Morgan began to undress himself, he started at the bottom, he succeeded then he began to undo his buttons on his top, he found this extremely difficult so I undid them for him. Morgan was using two hands to undress himself. When taking his top off he pulled his head out from under the top and then he got it stuck on his shoulders, he began to get anxious and I took it off for him. I would say Morgan found it very difficult.

---

2 Observations should be relevant to the chosen area(s) of development

The written accounts of the observations should relate to the chosen area(s) of development. You should record all the information that you observe that is to do with developmental ability. For example, if social development is being observed for two children, it is the interaction that takes place between the children that is important for that particular observation.

3 Observations should include a number of different methods of observation

If possible, you should include a number of different methods of observing the child/children in order to gain more marks. At the end of each observation, it may be useful to write two or three sentences as a conclusion to explain exactly what has been found out (see below). This will help when writing up the evaluation.

Conclusion

I would be very careful in choosing the same activity again for a two-year-old. I now believe it was too difficult. If I was doing it again I would make sure the child wasn't tired – Morgan hadn't had a rest in the afternoon, when normally he would have had a rest for an hour. I believe this didn't improve the situation.

Application of knowledge

You should work through the following stages.

1 Interpret observations to show understanding of the chosen development area(s)

You need to use the evidence gained in the observations on the development area(s) and to show you have understanding of what you have observed.

2 Use the research in the task analysis to apply knowledge

The research collected in the task analysis should be used in order to relate the theory to what has been seen in the observations (the practice). If appropriate, you should make references to and quote from certain research items.

3 Offer original thought and opinion

It is important that you provide your own thoughts and opinions when talking about what has been observed. This shows you understand the development you have seen in relation to your child.

4 Compare development with other children

A comparison with other children of some form should take place so that you can see how your child is progressing in relation to another child. If it is not possible to compare with another child of a similar age, a comparison with the textbook norm is acceptable (see below).

Application of knowledge

Morgan my two year old	Compared with another two year old
Morgan did succeed in undressing himself even though he found this very difficult. In several areas I had to help him	Compared to another two year old Morgan is at the average stage for undressing himself. Most two year olds either can't undress themselves or find it very difficult
Morgan can independently walk up the stairs safely but finds it difficult in coming down the stairs.	An average two year old can walk up and down the stairs by doing two feet per stair

Individual task: evaluation

The evaluation is on the whole of the individual task, so you should look through all your work before making any comments. You should work through the following stages.

1 Logical conclusions on what has been observed and found out

If conclusions have been added to the end of each of the observations, then this information can be included in this section. Marks can be credited for these conclusions wherever there is written evidence, e.g. at the end of the observations or in the evaluation. You need to be able to interpret any evidence collected in the execution and include it in this part of the evaluation.

2 Personal views about the outcome

Once again, personal opinion is important in this section. You should write about the outcome of your execution, using evidence to support your comments.

3 A review and assessment of your performance in all the work

You need to make comments about your task in relation to how you felt it had worked and what you have achieved. For example, perhaps you are very satisfied with how you carried out your research and the way it was presented in the task analysis, or perhaps more activities could have been covered in the development section to give more choice when making a selection to carry forward in the planning.

4 Reasons for any changes made to the plan

During the carrying out of the observations section, it is important that any changes to the plan are noted and recorded within the evaluation. These changes must be supported with reasons. For example, if an activity was planned and the child soon lost interest or would not co-operate, it may be that another activity was carried out that was not included in the original plan. This needs to be written up, giving appropriate reasons.

5 Strengths and weaknesses and reasons for these

You are required to write about the strengths and weaknesses of the task and to give an indication as to how they affected the outcome. For example, if the research has not been covered in sufficient detail or variety, this could have an effect on how well the application of knowledge is covered. Another example would be that detailed, careful, thorough planning provided you with useful activities to carry out with the child in the observations and the knowledge of what to look for in the development area(s). Successful observations would have an obvious affect on the final outcome of the task.

6 An assessment of the task title – was the choice relevant and effective in relation to the child/children?

The task title and the chosen area(s) of development should be referred to in this part of the evaluation. You should be able to say, using the evidence gained from the execution, if the choice of the title was appropriate and relevant to your child/children. The effectiveness of the title also needs to be considered. Have you found out what you intended to discover at the start of the task?

Written communication

The final area of the marking scheme in the evaluation is based on the presentation of the task, as well as spelling, punctuation, grammar and use of specialist terms. You should be aware at the start of the task that these factors will be assessed in the criteria. The evaluation is the area where continuous writing is likely to occur and where these marks are awarded (see below). However, the task as a whole will be looked at when awarding these marks.

I would have preferred to study a child who was a little older than William, perhaps about three years old, so that there could have been a wider choice of observations to choose from, but as I had no other child to observe I had to make do.

I am quite satisfied with my write-ups about the different developments and stages of progression because I feel that I have written short but concise notes.

I am pleased that I chose to study manipulative skills in particular because these linked closely with William's age and there were a lot of observations that I could plan that involved manipulative skills. With my task title I felt I didn't want to make it too specific because that would narrow down the types of activities for William, but by including the aspect of familiarity and favouritism it wasn't left too open-ended.

In the development and planning areas I made sure I researched well into the relevant stages of manipulative skills, as well as more general information on physical development.

I feel that I collected adequate information on William before I started to look at the development section.

I made sure that when I was planning the activities for the observations William either had already done each of them so I knew he was capable or that he should be able to do them at his age.

Having seen William's capabilities I would perhaps have added an observation using beads and cotton reels for threading. I didn't include this initially because from my first few visits I didn't think he would be able to do this.

I produced a logical plan which I tried to follow but didn't manage:

✦ On Visit 1 I observed William with building blocks as I had planned and found out some important points as planned.
✦ Visit 2 was supposed to be a drawing activity but at the last minute I had to chnage the time of the visit. The new time suited William's bedtime rather than doing a drawing activity.
✦ Visit 3 was supposed to involve Duplo but in order to try and get on track with my plan I got William to do some drawing.
✦ Visit 4 was supposed to be garden activities but the weather wasn't appropriate and eventually this observation was repeatedly postponed and William's mother preferred it if I didn't do this observation at all. Instead on this visit I got William to play again with the building blocks.
✦ Visit 7 was supposed to be modelling dough but when I arrived William was already playing with his Duplo and, as I hadn't already done the observation with Duplo, I decided that doing it on this occasion was best.
✦ I had planned for Visit 8 to be bedtime, but as I had already done this and not modelling dough I decided to do that instead.

I recorded my observations in a way which I felt was most appropriate for the types of observations I was carrying out. I didn't vary my methods of recording my evidence as much as I probably could have done. I did include a graph and a drawing but I felt that if I had used other methods, e.g. tick charts, I wouldn't have got as much information.

With William living only a few miles away it wasn't difficult for me to get to see him and his mother was very willing to co-operate. I was able to carry out all but one of my planned observations.

I found the write-ups of my visits difficult because I didn't want to repeat the information I'd already written in my task analysis. Also, the more observations I wrote up, the more I felt the content was becoming repetitive. Overall, though, I felt my write-ups provided me with the information I'd set out to get.

I think the activities I planned allowed me to see the changes as William was progressing. I achieved this by planning a variety of activities.

I enjoyed the task analysis section, writing about physical development in particular, because I prefer the theory side of this work.

I think I successfully interpreted my observations and I tried to relate this to my research into manipulative skills.

I managed to find a child to compare Wiliam with but found it difficult to observe much because Adam didn't know me and was obviously shy.

The importance of my work lies in the fact that I have showed an understanding of William's manipulative development and, therefore, feel that there is no one main important piece of work.

With my task title 'How do the fine manipulative actions of an eighteen-month-old develop and differ according to the object?' I have fulfilled my original intentions. I discovered that an eighteen-month-old can build a tower of nine blocks, do simple jigsaws and play with modelling dough and this is because the activities I chose to carry out in my observations were appropriate to the age of the child as well as being designed to give me the maximum information required in order to answer my task title.

Resource tasks

Resource tasks are split into three sections.

1 Planning

The resource task planning section should include details of what is to be carried out in the execution area. Regardless of the demands of the task, it is important that careful planning is carried out in order to help produce a successful execution. The plan should include (a) a logical plan of action and (b) a list of resources.

(a) A logical plan of action

A plan should cover every area that is going to be carried out in the execution (see diagram below).

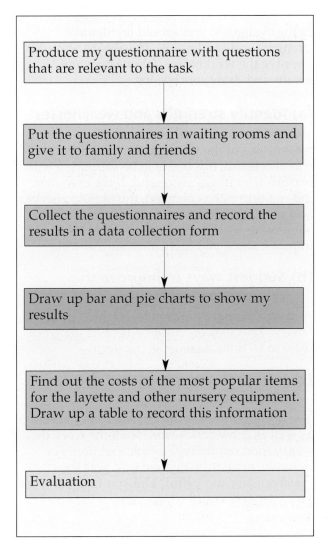

If the plan has as much detail as possible it allows you to carry out a successful execution. It should include details of what is going to be done, e.g. whether it is an investigative, task or a making task. The plan for an investigative task should include what is going to be looked at, what information is to be collected and an order of work. If a survey or questionnaire is to be used, this should also be included in the plan. Also, the group to be questioned should be identified. The plan for a making task – where you are going to produce an item such as a leaflet, a book or a snack – should include details of what is to be made, any relevant drawings/diagrams and how it is to be made, including a possible order of work.

(b) A list of resources

You need to include any resources to be used in order to carry out the task in the plan. This means a selection of sources where information can be found, e.g. textbooks, leaflets and people, as well as equipment required to carry out the task, e.g. materials or food. The work can be presented in any form and use ICT where appropriate.

2 Execution (carry out the planned task)

The execution area is split into two sections: (a) organization and (b) outcome.

(a) Organization

This includes:

+ carrying out the planned work
+ using a range of methods
+ organizing and using resources effectively and safely
+ responding to changes promptly
+ using a range of processes and techniques.

This section is where you carry out the task using the plan. You should be able to demonstrate a range of methods and processes/techniques, including ICT where appropriate. Any resources used should be organized efficiently and safely and any changes that are made to the plan should be recorded. Written evidence is required for the organization, e.g. how an item was made, and completed questionnaires, to show that you have carried out the task.

(b) Outcome

This includes:

---

1. Which of these items did you buy for your babies layette?
   - ❏ Vest
   - ❏ Stretchsuits
   - ❏ Cardigans
   - ❏ Socks
   - ❏ Booties
   - ❏ Mittens
   - ❏ Hat/Bonnet
   - ❏ Shawl
   - ❏ Babygro
   - ❏ Sleepsuits
   - ❏ Pramsuit
   - ❏ Snowsuit
   - ❏ Bibs

2. Which item did you find the most expensive? ....
   ....

3. Which nursery equipment did you buy for your baby?
   - ❏ Cot
   - ❏ Carry cot
   - ❏ Travel cot
   - ❏ Cradle
   - ❏ Blankets/Sheets
   - ❏ Mattress
   - ❏ Baby intercom
   - ❏ Pram
   - ❏ Pushchair
   - ❏ Buggy
   - ❏ Walking Reins
   - ❏ Baby Nest
   - ❏ Baby Carrier
   - ❏ Baby Cradle
   - ❏ High Chair
   - ❏ Car Seat
   - ❏ Baby Bath
   - ❏ Baby Bouncer
   - ❏ Playpen

4. Which item did you find the most expensive? ....
   ....

✦ producing of a quality outcome
✦ producing a range of detailed and accurate results.

The outcome is the result of the organization section. It may be something that has been produced, the results of a survey/questionnaire, etc. It is important that there is some evidence to support the marks awarded and this may be given in graphic evidence, especially where an item has been produced (see diagram opposite).

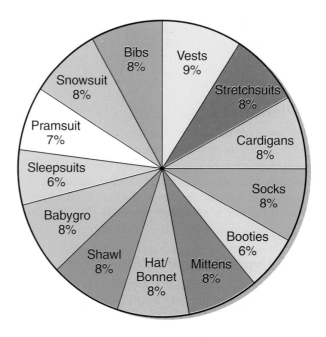

3 Evaluation

In the evaluation you should (a) identify strengths and weaknesses, (b) suggest ways to improve the weaknesses, (c) interpret any results and draw conclusions.

(a) Identify strengths and weaknesses

You need to pick out the strengths and weaknesses of the whole of the task. If the plan was successful, this needs to be supported with reasons why it was successful. If the execution did not turn out as planned, this should also be acknowledged. You are required to be critical about your work in a positive way to help you improve when you carry out a further task.

(b) Suggest ways to improve the weaknesses

Any weaknesses you have highlighted need to have suggestions on improvements if the work were to be done again.

(c) Interpret any results and draw conclusions

You need to interpret any results from the task as well as draw conclusions from the work that was carried out in the execution section. For example, in an investigative task, was the questionnaire successful? Did you find out what you intended to at the beginning of the task?

Glossary

abdomen – the part of the body called the stomach area

abortion – ending a pregnancy

abstention – saying 'no'

adoption – the legal process where adults become parents to children they have not given birth to

afterbirth – another term for the placenta

AIDS (Acquired Immune Deficiency Syndrome) – caused by the HIV virus

Alphafetoprotein (AFP) – a blood test for screening spina bifida

amino acids – small component parts of a protein

amniocentesis – a test using a hollow needle to remove amniotic fluid

amniotic sac – the foetus develops inside this sac, which is full of fluid

antenatal – before birth

artificial insemination – the injection of sperm into the uterus

attention deficit disorder – a disorder of children who cannot concentrate for periods of time

autism – children with autism find it difficult to communicate with others including their families

balanced diet – a diet that contains the right amount and proportions of nutrients

barrier methods – contraceptives that protect against STDs

birth canal – the uterus, cervix and the vagina form the birth canal

bonding – feelings of love and affection between parents and their baby

breaking of the waters – the amniotic sac breaks releasing the fluid

breech birth – when the legs or bottom are born first

British Standards Kitemark – a symbol, which indicates that a product has been tested to given standards

Caesarian section – an operation to remove a baby

cerebral palsy – a congenital condition that is caused by lack of oxygen shortly before or after birth

child benefit – an allowance paid to a parent of every child

ChildLine – an organization that offers confidential support and advice to children

Child Poverty Action Group – a pressure group that promotes action for the relief of poverty among children and families

child-resistant closures – used to prevent or delay a child opening a hazardous product

Child Support Agency – established in 1993 to help support lone parent families

chrionic villus sampling (CVS) – a test to remove a sample of the placenta

Citizens Advice Bureau – an organization that offers help and advice to people about a wide range of issues

cognitive – the development of understanding, reasoning and learning

co-habit – to live together without being married

colostrom – the first milk produced from the mother's breast after the birth of a baby

combined pill – contraceptive that contains two hormones

compulsory care – taking a child at risk into the care of the local authority

conception – the joining of an egg and a sperm

concepts – general ideas about life, for example heat, time, light, etc.

contraception – to prevent having a baby

contraceptive injection – injection of progesterone into the body

contractions – regular pains caused by the uterus contracting

contra-indication – a reaction to a vaccine

co-operative play – playing in a group

cot death – sudden death of a baby

creative play – the expression of feelings through materials, for example painting

cross-contamination – the transfer of bacteria from raw, contaminated food to other foods

crowning – the baby's head appears out of the vagina

deficiency diseases – diseases caused by a shortage of a nutrient

developmental screening tests – tests carried out regularly to assess a child's development

diaphragm (cap) with spermicide – covers the cervix and contains chemicals that kill sperm

dietary goals – targets set to try to improve the health of people

dietary reference values (DRVs) – the amount of nutrients needed by population groups

diet-related illnesses – diseases caused by the foods eaten in the diet

disability allowance – an allowance paid to help cover the cost of caring for a disabled child or adult

Down's syndrome – a genetic condition caused by having an extra chromosome in the cells

early intervention programmes – learning programmes, which are designed to speed up the development of children with special needs in the pre-school

egg donation – a woman donates an egg

embryo – the name given to the fertilized egg after implantation

embryo donation – an embryo is placed in another woman's uterus

entonox – nitrous oxide and oxygen provided through a mask

epidural anaesthetic – a fine tube put into the mother's lower back

episiotomy – a small cut to widen the vaginal opening

exploratory play – involves the senses, for example touching different textures on a play mat

extended family – a nuclear family extended by grandparents or other relations such as aunts or uncles

female condom (femidom) – lines the vagina before sexual intercourse

female sterilization – an operation where the fallopian tubes are cut

field social workers – social workers who visit individuals and families in their homes

fine manipulative skills – the precise use of the hands and fingers

foetus – the embryo becomes a foetus after eight weeks

fontanelle – the soft spot on top of a newborn baby's head

food intolerance – a reaction to a food or an ingredient in the food product

food poisoning or food borne disease – a disease caused by eating contaminated food

food preferences – the foods a child likes or dislikes

food refusal – when a child refuses to eat their food

forceps delivery – metal instruments that fit around the baby's head to help ease out during birth

formula milk – the name given to milks and milk powders designed for babies

foster care – when a child is looked after by adults other than their own family

gamete intra fallopian transfer (GIFT) – using a couple's own or donated egg/sperm

genes – contain information, for example hair and eye colour

genetic counseling – consulting an expert on hereditary diseases

Gingerbread – a support organization for lone parent families which offers practical help, contact and information

gross motor skills – the use of the large muscles of the body

hand-eye co-ordination skills – the ability to connect the movement of the hands with what the eyes can see

hazardous substance – a substance, which is a danger to a child, such as common household chemicals like bleach, anti-freeze, after-shave and lavatory cleaner

hormones – chemical messengers that travel through the bloodstream

housing benefit and council tax benefit – a benefit that assists in the costs of housing for families on low incomes

human immunodeficiency virus (HIV) – a virus passed on through sexual intercourse and bodily fluids

identical twins – when one fertilized egg splits into two individual embryos

imaginative play – using the imagination through play, for example playing shops

immunity – the body's ability to resist infection

immunization – to prevent a disease

immunized – protected against a disease

implantation – when the fertilized egg becomes attached to the uterus lining

implants – small tubes inserted under the skin

income support – a benefit for those whose income falls below a given level of money and are not working, or working less than sixteen hours a week

incubation period – the time between the original contact with the bacteria and the appearance of the first symptoms of the disease

induction – starting labour off artificially

infectious diseases – diseases caused by bacteria or viruses

infertility – the inability to conceive

intra cytoplasmic sperm injection (ICSI) – a single sperm is injected into an egg in a laboratory

intrauterine device (IUD) – a plastic and copper device that is fitted into the uterus

intrauterine system (IUS) – a plastic device that is fitted into the uterus

in vitro **fertilization (IVF)** – the egg is fertilized in a laboratory

jaundice – causes the skin and eyes to be tinged yellow

joining in play – watching other children play

kibbutz – communities, which are collective farms where individuals work to help and support all the community

labour – the process of giving birth

lactating – another word for breastfeeding

lanugo – fine downy hair covering the body of a foetus

layette – the first set of baby clothes

listeriosis – a rare disease caused by bacteria in certain foods

lone-parent families – families that have one parent, usually the mother, looking after the child or children

looked-after children – children who are cared for by the local authority

low birth weight baby – a full term baby weighing less than 2.5kg (5lbs)

macronutrient – nutrients that the body needs in large amounts

male condom – fits over the penis before sexual intercourse

male sterilization (vasectomy) – an operation where the sperm tubes are cut

manipulative play – the movement of the hands, for example threading beads

means tested – where the income of the family is compared with a standard amount of money to assess if they are in need of financial support

menstruation – a flow of blood that occurs monthly

micronutrients – nutrients that are needed in small quantities, such as vitamins and minerals

milestones – a way of assessing the progress of a child's development

miscarriage – an accidental ending of a pregnancy

mispronunciation – mistakes made when learning to pronounce words

modified or step families – other names for reconstituted families

natural family planning (NFP) – understanding your personal menstrual cycle (not using contraceptives)

nature – refers to a child's natural ability

non-identical twins – when two different sperms fertilize two eggs

non-verbal communication – a baby communicating without words

nurture – the way a child is stimulated and interacted with

nutrition – a study of the nutrients found in the foods in our diet

oestrogen – a female sex hormone

opportunity playgroups – specialist playgroups for children with special needs

ovulation – when an egg is released from an ovary

parallel play – playing beside another child

Parents Anonymous – an organization that offers information, support and help for parents and families

passport benefits – entitlement to other benefits

period – a term meaning flow of blood

Persona – a fertility device to predict fertile/infertile times during the menstrual cycle

pethidine – pain relief in the form of an injection

physical play – physical activities, for example running and climbing

placenta – an organ that provides nourishment and removes waste for the foetus

plaque – formed when bacteria in the mouth convert the sugar to an acid

postnatal – refers to the days and weeks immediately after the birth

pre-conceptual care – the health of a mother-to-be before conception

pregnancy – the time between conception and birth

premature baby – one born before thirty-seven weeks of pregnancy

pre-reading – a term used to describe the skills a child needs to have acquired before learning to read

progesterone – a female sex hormone

progesterone-only pill (POP) – contraceptive that contains one hormone

prop feeding – a dangerous practice of feeding a baby by propping up the bottle with a pillow

reconstituted families – families that have changed in structure and reformed in a new way

regress – go backwards in an area of development

relaxation and breathing exercises – natural childbirth techniques to relieve pain

respite care – a support system, which enables families of special needs children to have a break from caring for their special needs child

role-play – acting out adult roles, for example doctors and nurses

safety restraint – a device to keep a child safe when traveling

semen – a milky substance that contains sperm

sensory exploration – exploring using the senses, for example listening to different sounds

sexually transmitted diseases (STDs) – disease passed on through sexual intercourse

Shelter – an organization that campaigns on behalf of the homeless and those in poverty

show – a plug of mucus that comes away from the cervix

Siamese twins – when one fertilized egg does not split into two completely

sibling rivalry – a child feeling that a brother/sister may be receiving more attention than them

socialization – learning how to live in society, how to behave and act in different situations

social play – the way children play together, for example playing football

social security system – the support system set up by the government to provide benefits to those in need

spina bifida – an abnormality where the brain and spinal cord fail to develop properly

statutory support – support services that have to be provided by the local authority

sure start maternity grants – financial support which helps pay for the costs of a new baby, available as a single payment for families on low income

symptoms – the changes in the body, which show disease, such as spots

terminating – ending a pregnancy

testosterone – a male sex hormone

transcutaneous electrical nerve stimulation (TENS) – a gentle electrical current is passed through four pads attached to the back

umbilical cord – links the foetus to the placenta

unconditional love – love given freely by parents without conditions

universal benefits – benefits available to everyone entitled to receive them regardless of income, such as child benefit

vaccine – a substance which makes the body produce antibodies to fight infection

ventouse – a special cap connected to a suction pump fitted to the baby's head

verbal communication – talking

vernix – a greasy coating on the newborn baby's skin

weaning or mixed feeding – the change from liquid to solid food

Working Families' Tax Credit – a benefit to support families on low income but who are in employment and have at least one child

Index